BUT GOD CAN

HOW TO ~~STOP STRIVING AND~~ LIVE PURPOSEFULLY AND ABUNDANTLY

Becky Kiser

W PUBLISHING GROUP

AN IMPRINT OF THOMAS NELSON

Published in Nashville, Tennessee, by W Publishing, an imprint of Thomas Nelson.

Thomas Nelson titles may be purchased in bulk for educational, business, fundraising, or sales promotional use. For information, please email SpecialMarkets@ThomasNelson.com.

Unless otherwise noted, Scripture quotations are taken from the ESV® Bible (The Holy Bible, English Standard Version®). Copyright © 2001 by Crossway, a publishing ministry of Good News Publishers. Used by permission. All rights reserved.

Scripture quotations marked AMP are taken from the Amplified® Bible (AMP). Copyright © 2015 by The Lockman Foundation. Used by permission. www.lockman.org

Scripture quotations marked MSG are taken from The Message. Copyright © 1993, 2002, 2018 by Eugene H. Peterson. Used by permission of NavPress. All rights reserved. Represented by Tyndale House Publishers, Inc. a division of Tyndale House Ministries.

Scripture quotations marked NASB are taken from the New American Standard Bible® (NASB). Copyright © 1960, 1962, 1963, 1968, 1971, 1972, 1973, 1975, 1977, 1995, 2020 by The Lockman Foundation. Used by permission. www.lockman.org

Scripture quotations marked NIV are taken from The Holy Bible, New International Version®, NIV®. Copyright © 1973, 1978, 1984, 2011 by Biblica, Inc.® Used by permission of Zondervan. All rights reserved worldwide. www.Zondervan.com. The "NIV" and "New International Version" are trademarks registered in the United States Patent and Trademark Office by Biblica, Inc.®

Scripture quotations marked NKJV are taken from the New King James Version®. Copyright © 1982 by Thomas Nelson. Used by permission. All rights reserved.

Scripture quotations marked NLT are taken from the Holy Bible, New Living Translation. © Copyright 1996, 2004, 2015 by Tyndale House Foundation. Used by permission of Tyndale House Ministries, Carol Stream, Illinois 60188. All rights reserved.

Scripture quotations marked TPT are taken from The Passion Translation®. Copyright © 2017, 2018 by Passion & Fire Ministries, Inc. Used by permission. All rights reserved. ThePassionTranslation.com.

ISBN 978-1-4003-3577-0 (audiobook)
ISBN 978-1-4003-3576-3 (ePub)
ISBN 978-1-4003-3575-6 (TP)

Library of Congress Control Number: 2023945441

Printed in the United States of America

24 25 26 27 28 LBC 5 4 3 2 1

To my girls: Karis, Moriah, and Chandler

My greatest hope and prayer is for you to fully know and live out all I wrote within these pages. The world will pressure you to do it all and be anything. Take that pressure off! The truth is that you can't do it all, nor are you meant to be just anything. My loves, you are only meant to be yourself. So don't waste time striving to be anyone else or to fulfill others' expectations for you. God's way is always better.

Go and discover your purpose; then live it out to the fullest! Once you make that commitment, you will experience true and lavish abundance. I will always be here for you—as your biggest cheerleader, listener, counselor, guide, advocate, and bestie-for-the-restie.

I love you so much—no matter what!
XO,

Mom

I have no clue where to go or what to do

I'm completely over~~it~~

I'm not enough

I'm all alone

That is

CONTENTS

Part 3: Finding Your Way in The Wilderness

BEFORE YOU START: A LETTER FROM BECKY

I'm sitting just feet from one of the most significant women in my life as I write this letter to you. I'm watching her chest slowly rise and fall, and my heart breaks a bit more as each pause between is longer than the last. There are many more devastating trials in the world than this loss I am currently walking through. Even so, this one hurts.

I decided to read through the draft of this book right now because I need it to be truly helpful. After my mamaw's yearlong fight against cancer, I'm at her bedside for these final weeks of her life. I'm holding these words against what I'm walking through to see if they carry weight. I need them to carry weight.

I don't know what you are walking through at this moment—whether it's a season of a small or a significant trial, a season of joy and celebration, or a little bit of both. Whatever place you find yourself in, know that you are welcome here—all you are and all you are going through is safe. Too often we struggle to acknowledge that what we are going through matters because we have just enough perspective to know it could be worse. We shove things down and do what "good Christian women" are "supposed" to do; we plaster on the smile and prop up the facade that everything is okay. We are not trying to deceive anyone; we just don't know a better way.

That's why I'm sharing this message. Because we—you, me, and all our friends and family—need a better way. I'm praying for you and believing this time will be pivotal and marked as "before I opened and did the work within these pages" and "after." Neither of us has a clue what God is about to do in your life and heart, *but God can* do absolutely anything; of this I am certain. Friend, I believe in faith with you that God can and will astound you. I say "with" you because even if you don't fully believe that He can do miracles in, through, and around you, you had enough faith to pick up this book. That means you haven't given up hope yet, and I'm proud of you for that—and really, really expectant!

Here's the first bit of good news: you don't need to have a lot of faith. Jesus said, "if you have faith like a grain of mustard seed, you will say to this mountain, 'Move from here to there,' and it will move, and nothing will be impossible for you" (Matthew 17:20). We are excellent at believing this for everyone else in our lives. You can probably think of more than a handful of people you believe this for now. But turn that verse toward yourself this time. If you have faith as tiny as a mustard seed (which is smaller than the letter *o* on this page), you could move whatever mountain is in front of you with just a word.

I don't know what mountain (or maybe mountains) you are staring at, but I feel confident there is one before you. Right now I wish it were just a couch cushion that separated us instead of a page. I've prayed repeatedly that this book would feel like you are at my house having a very real conversation with a bestie/big sis/mom/coach/whatever you need right now. I'll wrap you in a big bear hug when you walk through the door. (I won't apologize for the mess piled at the bottom of the stairs because I cannot get my kids to take their things upstairs for the life of me!) I'll ask which flavor of coffee and creamer you want (or if you are more of a tea person, I have all kinds of options for you too). Then we will find a cozy spot on my couch, and I'll offer you a fuzzy blanket, look you in the eyes, and listen as you tell me about your mountain.

> **NOTE:** This is one of many times I will ask you to pause and reflect. If possible, take a minute and do so each time. If you aren't able to pause now, mark the page to come back to later. Let this be where you find the freedom you want—there is purpose in all of it.

Take a moment to tell me about your mountain. What in your life feels overwhelming? What feels heavy or hard? Where is your confidence shot or insecurity reigning? What brings you to tears quickly or makes you want to pretend it's not your reality?

Oh, Friend, I'm sorry for everything you wrote down or thought through. I'm sorry for the pain these things have caused and the fear that grips you. I'm sorry if you've ever felt you needed to act like you were okay when you weren't. I wish so much that life were less challenging than it has been.

I'm reading through the book of Job right now, and I've never been more confident that the Father creates space for us to grieve. Sometimes we feel pressure to say "I'm good" when we're hurting or reply "I'm blessed" when we see our mountains that look more like hills next to what others are facing. Most of us are carrying something—whether it's deeply painful or something uncertain.

Jesus can handle all of it. You can bring your hurt, fear, insecurity, anxiety, unknowns, shame—any and all of it—to Jesus. And you can bring it to this moment, our place together on the couch too. You are safe here. Together we will find our way to freedom.

In *The Message* paraphrase of Matthew 11:28–30, Jesus said, "Are you tired? Worn out? Burned out on religion? Come to me. Get away with me and you'll recover your life. I'll show you how to take a real rest. Walk with me and work with me—watch how I do it. Learn the unforced rhythms of grace. I won't lay anything heavy or ill-fitting on you. Keep company with me and you'll learn to live freely and lightly." How good does that sound—living freely and lightly? That's my hope for you and what I believe is possible!

This mountain you are facing or will face isn't your roadblock. This mountain isn't a closed door. While it will mark you as all parts of our journeys do, this mountain doesn't define you. The Lord will use this mountain just as He uses all things for good (Romans 8:28). It's why James said, "Count it all joy, my brothers, when you meet trials of various kinds, for you know that the testing of your faith produces steadfastness. And let steadfastness have its full effect, that you may be perfect and complete, lacking in nothing" (1:2–4). For reasons we may not understand, God is using all that you've walked through in the past and all you are currently walking through in the present to perfect and complete you so that you will lack nothing. I completely understand that, depending on what you are going through, my last statement may make you want to roll your eyes in disbelief. I get it—remember, I'm currently right there with you. *But God can.* Give Him a chance to prove your skepticism wrong as you find a new way.

The second bit of good news is that it's not impossible for that mountain to move! The verse you read at the beginning of this letter tells us that. Please, dear friend, catch the critical word *nothing*. *No thing.* That is why we can add "but God can" to every objection the Enemy wants to make us believe about ourselves or our lives. Not one single thing is impossible for your Father!

Return to what you wrote on the mountains and write "But God Can" over them. Then place your hand on top of those words, surrender them and yourself to God, and ask Him to do the impossible.

Finally, receive this prayer over you from me:

Father, thank You for my sweet friend holding these pages in her hand. I don't know the mountains before her, but You do. You know. You see. May she know that to her core—that You know, see, and love her more than she could ever imagine. Jesus, give her a mustard seed of faith right now that You can do anything. In Your name, I ask that You protect her mind from any temptation to doubt the work You will do in her heart and life. Please help her to feel safe here and to work her way vulnerably through the concepts, questions, and challenges. Give her discipline to pick up this book. Draw her to it when all the distractions of life come up. Help her to trust You as she goes through these pages. Show her the "unforced rhythms of grace" when she trusts in You, not herself. Lord, I ask that You will move mountains in her life. Perform a miracle! We know You can. We are asking that You would! In Jesus' mighty name, I pray. Amen.

Before we start, I want to give you a few tips since this book will be structured slightly different than others you've read.

Tip 1: Give Yourself Grace, but Not Too Much

I don't know about you, but I have at least eight books on my nightstand that I hope to finish soon, and many more on a shelf in another room. You can probably relate. You had every intention of reading a book you know would have been helpful for you, but you never did. Give yourself some grace! Today is a new day, and this is a new book. But don't give yourself too much grace! Don't redefine grace to mean you get away with everything. Instead, know that grace is what Jesus gives you when you return to Him. And grace is what we extend to ourselves when we realize we're off track and ready to return to what is best. This won't be easy. One million things will come up to distract you—let's fight those together!

What might be your top distractions?

Identifying what will tempt you away from reading and processing this book now will set you up for success! (For example, I would say: my phone, Instagram, email, news app, and my to-do list.)

What can you do to stop or limit that distraction?

Now, identify a solution for each of the distractions you listed above. You know these distractions won't magically disappear just because you identified them. You are going to have to do something about them! (Example: I will put my phone in the other room while I'm reading the book or put it on silent mode and turn it upside down.)

Now I will ask you to do something you won't want to do if you are anything like me. Most of us can hardly RSVP to things within a reasonable time frame. Our society is known to avoid commitment, but I will ask you to make one anyway. When I was in high school, I had a devotional that asked readers to sign on an actual dotted line before beginning the book so they would commit to not quitting and stick with the book for thirty days. You know what? I did that devo in thirty-ish days and have repeated it several times. I still remember that commitment and book two and a half decades later. Why? Because when we commit to something instead of going in with an "I'll see" attitude, we are available for change. I urge you to do the same with this book.

Will you commit to reading this book?

If yes, then sign your name below. (Tip: Set a goal to read a certain amount by a certain time.)

_____

Tip 2: Find at Least Three Friends to Read with You

The best way to stick with a book (or anything in life) is to do it with others! Who are some women you like, respect, believe in, and trust? Invite them to go through this book with you.

What friends could you invite to do this with you?

(Cross off their names once you've reached out to them. Do this ASAP!)

Y'all can hold each other accountable to keep reading. Or, since each chapter includes questions to process and challenges to apply what you're reading, you may want to form a book club. You can do this in person or virtually—whatever works best. Your friends and family all have their own mountains. They desperately want the Father to show them the "but God can" He has planned for their lives. So why not invite them on this journey with you?

Tip 3: Complete the Prompts, Questions, and Challenges

This book is interactive and often structured to feel like an in-person coaching session. You will get so much more out of it if you take the time to complete each part. If you are reading and don't have time to pause and reflect, mark the page to return to that prompt later. Push yourself to dig deep during those times. And if you are doing this with others, share what you are processing. Be open to letting your friends challenge you, and take the time to encourage them as well.

At the end of each chapter, you will see three sections:

1. **PRAY:** Let's wrap each chapter in prayer! Prayer is one of the best ways we acknowledge we can't *but God can*. I've provided you with a prayer you can use, or you can pray on your own—whatever you prefer.
2. **PROCESS:** I provide questions at the end of each chapter.

These are optional but are a great way to further process things on your own and with others.

3. **HEARERS & DOERS CHALLENGE:** James 1:22 says, "Be doers of the word, and not hearers only, deceiving yourselves." *Hearers & Doers* is the name of my podcast because James 1:22 is a core verse for me. Many of us have become ardent consumers of information—constantly taking in books, blogs, podcasts, news, and social media content. All that has desensitized us to God's truth, which we sometimes treat as another outlet of consumerism. James said, however, that we shouldn't just hear the truth but do something about it. We won't just be consumers because, at the end of each chapter, I'll guide you in how to apply what you've learned.

Tip 4: Stay Expectant

I hope the visual of your mountain is already more apparent, and I believe you will see it move as your perspective shifts. Don't miss it! Be expectant! Hebrews 11:1 says, "Now faith is the assurance of things hoped for, the conviction of things not seen." You may not see your mountain moving yet; just hold on to that mustard seed of faith that it will! We have just gotten started, my friend! Watch the impossible happen before your eyes because this isn't a trick or gimmick. Instead, this is surrendering your expectations and hopes to Jesus with open hands. That includes submitting how, when, and where you want that mountain to move. God told us that all things are possible. So fix your eyes on the Father as He takes your mountain of a story and adds a "but God can" to it.

I can't wait to see what God does as He helps you find your identity in Him, brings much-needed healing, helps you build trust in

Him, and gives you the courage to go in the ways He has for you. He has plans for you—very, very good plans. Let's chase after Him together!

XO,

Becky Kiser

I have no clue where to go or what to do

I'm completely overwhelmed

I'm not enough

I'm all alone

PART 1

FORGET THE FORMER THINGS

Forget the former things; do not dwell on the past. See, I am doing a new thing! Now it springs up; do you not perceive it? I am making a way in the wilderness and streams in the wasteland.

ISAIAH 43:18–19 (NIV)

Sometimes we are so intent on moving forward that we refuse to look back. We think, *What's the point? It doesn't change anything.* But a lifetime of counseling has taught me that reflecting on our experiences has great value. Both learning and healing from the past are essential to living a "but God can" life. That is what we are about to do—learn and heal as we reflect. But we won't stay stuck in the past. In Isaiah 43 we discover that we won't realize God is doing a new thing, nor will we find our way, until we "forget the former things" and stop dwelling on our past. Some of us are stuck looking back, making it impossible to move forward. That all changes right now. I'm so proud of you, so very expectant for you!

1

OUR "FAILURES"

Don't be afraid to fail.

Paw Paw Kiser (my husband, Chris's, grandfather)

Every day you are faced with a thought that isn't true: *You aren't enough*, which somehow makes you a failure. You experience it from the moment you wake up until you go to bed. It's one, often quiet, attack after another. You carry that *F* like it's your personal scarlet letter, believing a lie that you don't have what it takes.

You feel stuck—in shame, carpool lines, broken relationships, dead-end jobs, unfulfilled dreams, and unforgiveness. You may have felt this way for so long that you can't see another way, but you still desperately hope for one. You don't want to go through the motions—smiling on Sundays at church and projecting seemingly perfect images of your life, all while knowing you're missing your purpose. You can't seem to get off the proverbial hamster wheel, going round and round to nowhere. You are ready for your story to change; you want to believe you can live more significantly, leading a life filled with freedom and purpose. To call this thought spiral an attack feels too strong because you are mature enough to know that this is life and life isn't easy.

When we see ourselves as failures, we are looking at ourselves in a way inconsistent with God's view of us. My experience has been that many institutions that teach us how to live as Christians, especially as Christian women, have taught us to look down on ourselves and call it humility. We are going to heal that, my friend!

I want to share a popular verse with you that often appears on bumper stickers and coffee mugs. However, let's go a little further than the ever-popular verse 11.

> I know what I'm doing. I have it all planned out—plans to take care of you, not abandon you, plans to give you the future you hope for. When you call on me, when you come and pray to me, I'll listen. When you come looking for me, you'll find me. Yes, when you get serious about finding me and want it more than anything else, I'll make sure you won't be disappointed. . . . I'll turn things around for you. I'll bring you back . . . home to the place from which I sent you. . . . You can count on it. (Jeremiah 29:11–14 MSG)

When I became a Christian at sixteen and first heard verse 11, I felt like it was slightly taunting, almost like God was saying, *Ha! Ha! I know, and you don't!* I didn't understand the character of God then— that He is a good Father who only gives good gifts (Matthew 7:11). Once I read the full context of this verse, I got it! It wasn't that God knew and I didn't. Instead, God was giving us the best invitation ever. God was so good to tell us, *Hey! Do you want to know everything? Come to Me. Talk with Me. I can't wait to tell you. Oh, it's so good!*

We've heard countless times, "You go, girl! You got this! You can do anything!" Let me tell you, I am here for that. As a champion of women and a life coach, I believe in speaking life into one another. However,

I've learned that when pressed, those self-help mantras, while encouraging now, often fall flat under pressure. You've likely experienced this too. You've read the books, attended the conferences, listened to the podcasts, and resolved to think differently about yourself. You believe, if even for a moment, that you are finally free and capable of anything.

Then life happens, and you no longer feel so powerful. You get dumped and find yourself alone, or your marriage is struggling . . . again. You get passed up for that promotion or get stuck in the mundane rhythm of your day. You are bored or overstimulated. Medical diagnoses rock your world, or your bank account doesn't look how you thought it would by now. The person you thought was your friend betrayed you, or you've just never found your people. And that's just what's going on externally. It isn't even considering what's happening in your mind or your heart.

I know life isn't all bad; for many of you, it isn't even primarily bad. I won't propose resigning, defeated by life's heavy or challenging parts. Instead, we will find freedom from the heavy, because whether it's here now or coming soon, it's a part of life we simply can't escape. Isaiah 43:2 shoots it to us straight: "When you pass through the waters, I will be with you; and through the rivers, they shall not overwhelm you; when you walk through fire you shall not be burned, and the flame shall not consume you." Note that it says "when," because fires and floods will come—it's not an *if* but a *when*. I hope you will discover the truth that will be your life vest when those waters rise and your fire hydrant when those flames burn bright. Remember that our Father says you will not be overwhelmed or burned.

Always a skeptic and realist, I struggle to believe we won't be overwhelmed or burned because most of us have experienced both. *Overwhelm* means "to cover over completely: submerge; to overcome by superior force or numbers; to overpower in thought or feeling."[1] You may *feel* overwhelmed, but you have not been truly overwhelmed.

I remember hearing the song "King of My Heart" for the first time. As they repeated the chorus, "You are good, good, oh," it was as if I had been punched in the gut, and the breath left my lungs. While those leading and singing around me seemed to feel those words deeply, tears stung my eyes because I couldn't relate. The song continued, "You're never gonna let, never gonna let me down."[2] If I'm honest, God has let me down more than once. What happens when we look at our life, or parts of our life, and wonder how He let that happen or if things will ever get better?

Together we will look at a number of "failures" found throughout the Bible. But we will also examine our own "failures," and you will learn that I am the queen of failures. I feel like my whole life has been two steps forward, one step back (and sometimes eighteen steps back).

I went to Camp Well with the Well Summit a year ago, and it was one of the most transformative things I've ever done. Camp Well is a weeklong retreat in a Colorado mountain valley where you deal with your junk and take steps toward freedom to become and do what God has called you to be. One of the things that makes Camp Well especially game-changing is that you do prework before you go so that you are ready to hit the ground running when you get there. One of those activities absolutely broke me. Jenn Jett Barrett, the founder of Camp Well, had us map out our peaks (good things) and valleys (hard things). We were supposed to start at our earliest memory and record our peaks and valleys up to the present time and mark how high or low they ranked. I must confess, I put this part off until the last minute on my plane ride to the retreat.

I'm an Enneagram 3, which means my greatest fear in life is being a failure or worthless. (You will see through this book how Satan has had a field day trying to take me out with that root fear!)

That also explains why I put this project off until the last minute: I didn't want to acknowledge my valleys because I perceived them all as failures, even though they weren't all my fault. But I did the work because I'm also an overachiever and couldn't show up with half a packet filled out. And what God did next was break me in seat 23D with my tray table wobbling as I scribbled my peaks and valleys across my page.

It took the whole flight to map out. I held nothing back. And then I just stared at that page. I realized why I felt like I'd been on a roller coaster—because I had. As I connected the dots, I could finally see the drastic turns, from the highest highs to the lowest lows. The pain I didn't even realize I felt made sense—I had become numb from self-protection. I had stopped trusting myself for what seemed like justifiable reasons, but looking at the bigger picture, I saw something different. I started to believe there could be a "but God" coming that could change everything or at least some things.

Now it's your turn! I won't ask you to map out your whole life of peaks and valleys, but I want you to reflect on your failures or valleys and contrast them with some of your highs or mountaintops. Maybe these things don't rank as personal failures, but you still feel as though they might disqualify you, or you feel hurt or insecure because of them. For example, I've believed that I am automatically disqualified from being a writer because I have no clue what a semicolon does and only know how to write in run-on sentences. (That's obviously not true.)

We all perceive a thousand big and little failures to be true about ourselves. Below you'll find space to process yours. If you can, do this now. If you can't, promise yourself you will do it. You need to do it before you can freely move forward! Add in your highs as well. It's good to see the balance of both.

BUT GOD CAN

Track your failures/valleys and highs/mountaintops across this page.

Using this line, mark off your ages from as young as you remember until your current age. Then give yourself time, work through each phase and stage of your life, and record any significant failures or ones you can recall.

OUR "FAILURES"

Let me take this moment to reassure you that you are loved, you are safe here, and I'm proud of you. You are doing hard work, which will usher in freedom you've never known. You only need a mustard seed of faith, remember? God is moving mountains! He is using every single failure to bring about the good plans He is working out (Jeremiah 29:11).

My greatest hope for you is that by the time you turn the last page of this book, you will know that all the parts of your story that have always felt like failures instead demonstrate that God is weaving a greater story. On your own, you can't, *but God* absolutely *can*! He has made you stronger as you've faced countless trials—some brought on by sin but many brought on by life.

Putting self-help gimmicks to the side, let's hear two essential truths that Jesus said: "I am the way, and the truth, and the life. No one comes to the Father except through me" (John 14:6). And "The thief comes only to steal and kill and destroy. I came that they may have life and have it abundantly" (John 10:10). Did you catch that? Jesus is the way, and He doesn't just want life for you—He wants you to experience *abundant* life. He sees those "failures." He is ready to add "but God can" to them so you can experience the purpose-filled, abundant life He has planned for you.

As we wrap up this chapter, I don't want you to sit too long in these failures. They are worth acknowledging and grieving so you can learn from them. But let's not forget that our God can do absolutely anything with our failures. This isn't a "name it and claim it" book. I simply don't buy into the mentality of "if you build it, they will come." But I believe God can do anything with your life—beyond what you can ask or imagine. Your failures don't disqualify you; they bring God greater glory! I will likely quote this verse so much that I hope you will have it memorized before you've turned the last page: "Three times I pleaded with the Lord about this, that it should leave me. But he said to me, 'My grace is sufficient for you, for my power is made perfect in weakness.' Therefore I will boast all the more gladly of my weaknesses, so that the power of Christ may rest upon me. For the sake of Christ, then, I am content with weaknesses, insults, hardships, persecutions, and calamities. For when I am weak, then I am strong" (2 Corinthians 12:8–10). Our weaknesses give God the opportunity to show off His power!

The context of this verse is Paul pleading for the Lord to remove the "thorn" in his flesh. We don't know what it was, but he repeatedly begged God to remove it. I wonder if you have done something similar. How often have we hidden in shame over our "failures" or begged God to make a different way? I don't know why God has allowed some of what He has allowed in your life. I'm sorry for your pain. The hope-filled news in all of this is that the weaker we are, the stronger we become because of God's power! We can't, *but God can*!

I don't know what you've been trying to do in your own strength. I don't know what mountains are before you. But I know that when you stop trying to move a mountain yourself, you get to watch a God who created the entire world and all that fills it, parted the sea, raised the dead, walked on water, healed with just a word, multiplied a few fish to feed thousands, and did countless other things, do a mighty work in your life.

I want to ask you to do one more thing as an act of surrender.

Write "But God" over those failures you listed.
As you did with your mountains in my letter at the beginning of this book, do the same with that list of failures. This is a visual reminder of faith and trust in God.

I'm so proud of you for working through this chapter. I won't sugarcoat it: the steps toward lasting change aren't always easy. *But*

God. Friend, God has wonderful things planned for you. I want to commission you with the exact words Moses shared with Joshua as he was about to enter the promised land:

> I will be with you. I will not leave you or forsake you. Be strong and courageous. . . . Only be strong and very courageous, being careful to do according to all the law that Moses my servant commanded you. Do not turn from it to the right hand or to the left, that you may have good success wherever you go. This Book of the Law shall not depart from your mouth, but you shall meditate on it day and night, so that you may be careful to do according to all that is written in it. For then you will make your way prosperous, and then you will have good success. Have I not commanded you? Be strong and courageous. Do not be frightened, and do not be dismayed, for the LORD your God is with you wherever you go. (Joshua 1:5–9)

Are you ready? Let's go!

Pray

Father, thank You for letting me acknowledge my lows. It's refreshing that I don't have to pretend to be "blessed" or have it all together with You. Forgive me for believing that You have let me down instead of believing You are good like that song says. Help me to believe in and see Your goodness. Help me trust that You have truly good plans. Free me from believing that the hard things that have happened in my life and my mistakes mean I'm a failure. I don't want to be stuck in shame anymore! Give me hope that You will use my failures for good! Help me to trust that a miracle is coming.

Process

1. How does the new perspective on Jeremiah 29:11–14 help you see God's intentions and desires for you?
2. When you look at your list of "failures," how does it feel to see "But God" over them?
3. When you read in 2 Corinthians 12:8–10 that even Paul felt weak and realized it was an opportunity for God to get more glory and show His power, how does that convict or encourage you? Can you think of a time when you've experienced something similar?

Hearers & Doers Challenge

I invite you to come out of hiding. Identify how you have put up a facade with your failures. Then write a few realistic steps of how you can come out of hiding. Finally, go back to that list of failures, and if you can, write one way God has already used a failure to show His glory and power.

_____

_____

YOU'VE BEEN LIED TO

Just because someone says something is true doesn't mean that it is. Even if you wanna believe them. Even if you keep believing them. Even if they believe it themselves. In the end, you just have to admit that they're lying and change your own path.

Amy Bendix, *The Punisher*

When I was a kid, it was common for kids to be teased about having a crush (as if this would ever get a kid to open up about their crushes). I remember going to lunch with one of our closest family friends after church, and this situation came up. One of the siblings revealed that her brother, Trevor, had a crush. He promptly denied it. To which all of us at the table immediately started saying, "Ooooohhhhh, Trevor has a cruuu-ussshhhhh!" I can still hear and vividly see Trevor's response. He got up from his seat, stormed around the table, and screamed with the fervor of a warrior's battle cry, "*Liiiiiaaaarrrr! You're lying!*" This is the exact intensity I hope we all take as we read this chapter. I hope you can clearly see the lies you've believed and that you will learn how to scream back at the liar. Because the Enemy is, in fact, a liar. I pray that you'd become adamant and audacious in fighting for what is true.

One of my favorite Bible verses is Genesis 2:25: "The man and his wife were both naked and were not ashamed." I know it's kind of weird to be on my list of favorite verses, but here's why: what freedom they had—to be naked and unashamed! I don't know many women who could say this, do you? Adam and Eve knew a freedom most of us couldn't fathom. They were stripped bare yet didn't express a shred of shame. *Unashamed* is defined as "being without guilt, self-consciousness, or doubt."[1] Can you imagine a life without guilt, not a hint of self-consciousness, and where doubt doesn't exist? This is why the garden was perfection, until it wasn't.

In Genesis 3 we meet the serpent, who is said to be "more crafty than any other beast" (v.1). Other translations describe the serpent as "shrewdest" (NLT), "more crafty (subtle, skilled in deceit)" (AMP), "more clever" (MSG), and "more cunning" (NASB, NKJV). The serpent, who is Satan, was out to trick. We often think lies will be blatant, but we forget that Satan isn't like a kid who has just stolen a cookie and has the chocolate smeared across his face as he adamantly says he never ate a cookie. No, Satan is crafty, shrewd, subtle, skilled in deceit, clever, and cunning. I want to share a few other verses about Satan, the liar:

"The thief [Satan] comes only to steal and kill and destroy" (John 10:10).
"There is no truth in him [Satan]. When he lies, he speaks out of his own character, for he is a liar and the father of lies" (John 8:44).
"Your adversary the devil prowls around like a roaring lion, seeking someone to devour" (1 Peter 5:8).

Satan is *really* good at lying to you because of how intentionally deceptive he is. He will confuse your thoughts to where you don't know what's him, yourself, or even God. He intends to steal, kill, and destroy your time, relationships, purpose, emotions, and all the other good things God has placed in your life. He isn't just a liar; he is the Father of Lies—no one is better than him at twisting the truth or blatantly lying. He prowls around, solely intending to devour us. I don't mean to be dramatic, nor do we need to be fearful or discouraged. With this insight, we are no longer ignorant but ready to learn how to fight back when Satan slithers up to our ears, whispering lies.

Let's return to the garden to witness the first recorded lie ever. Even though it's hard for us to fully imagine or relate to, remember that Eve was a woman who was totally without shame and walked with God where she could sense His presence and hear His voice. Satan warmed her up, as he often does, by twisting what God said in Genesis 3:1: "Did God actually say, 'You shall not eat of any tree in the garden?'" Satan intends to confuse us so we don't know what is true and what is a lie. The truth is that God, in His goodness, only restricted Adam and Eve from one tree.

We know that Satan is referred to as a "roaring lion, seeking someone to devour" (1 Peter 5:8). The image I first had was of a giant lion standing on top of a big rock, roaring loudly for all to hear with his prey cowering beneath him. However, when a lion prowls around its prey, it scrunches low to the ground, undetected as the prey unknowingly goes about its day. These massive and powerful animals move slowly, waiting for the ideal moment. This is how Satan was with Eve, slowly prowling toward her, twisting and confusing the truth to where she didn't even notice what was happening. At first it seemed like Satan's attempts weren't working, as Eve corrected Satan that it wasn't all the trees but just the one they couldn't eat from. But then we learn in Genesis 3:4 that the Father of Lies was on the right track to steal, kill, and destroy the unashamed life Eve knew, blurring her truth one whisper at a time. Eve took what was true but allowed the truth to be twisted by saying that God said they couldn't even touch the tree or they'd die. His cunning plan was starting to work.

Satan had confused Eve about what God said. Next he wanted to cause her to question who God was. "You will not surely die. For God knows that when you eat of it your eyes will be opened, and you will be like God" (Genesis 3:4–5). Lions aren't cowards; they don't stay low to the ground once they see that their prey is vulnerable. They become fierce and ferocious as they attack and devour their prey.

It's not that Eve didn't stand a chance; she'd allowed herself to become vulnerable to attacks, letting the Enemy get too close. What was once clearly true had become fuzzy. This paved the way to believing a lie and taking action that changed her entire unashamed life. In Genesis 3:6–7 we see what happened next: "She took of its fruit and ate, and she also gave some to her husband who was with her, and he ate. Then the eyes of both were opened, and they knew that they were naked. And they sewed fig leaves together and made themselves loincloths." Satan had Eve's attention. She changed everything with one seemingly simple bite.

Eve had walked without shame in the garden with full access to God. We know that her freedom in the garden allowed her to sense, see, and experience God's presence and His voice. Yet with one bite innocence disappeared as shame took its place. Adam and Eve were immediately aware of their nakedness and tried to fix things by sewing fig leaves to cover themselves. Then they heard God in the garden and tried to hide. Up to this moment, all they had known was freedom. Now they knew shame.

God asked a question: "Where are you?" (3:9). It wasn't that He didn't know—He's God! To me, this is like when I used to play hide-and-seek with my girls when they were little. They'd hide behind a curtain, and I could clearly see their shoes poking out and hear their stifled giggles. But I would pretend I couldn't find them so they could get more out of the moment. Pretending I couldn't find them wasn't because I didn't know where they were. God, our good Father, was being a daddy to Adam and Eve. While this wasn't a giggly game of hide-and-seek, it was a Father's way of loving His children as best He could in a life-altering moment.

God constantly seeks us out, whether we want to be found or not. The question was to allow Adam and Eve an opportunity to admit what had happened and invite them back into a relationship with Him. They replied that they were naked, so they hid, to which God replied with another question: "Who told you that . . . ?" (3:11).

Notice something about God: He is God, the all-powerful God. Hadn't He warned Adam and Eve in Genesis 2:17 that they would "surely die" if they ate from the tree? And yet here they were, very much alive. I hope this encourages you—God isn't out to smite you but to restore a relationship with you. We must address the lies and hiding before we get to the restoration in our lives.

I'm a life coach, and the work I am all about is helping people move forward and do so with overflowing faith and optimism. I don't love looking back, and I don't love anything that feels negative. But let me assure you—this has been the most positive thing I've done for myself and my relationship with Jesus, even though it's not a fun process.

Next, we will list the lies of Satan that we believe. This process, especially if it's new to you, can feel awkward at first. While we are very familiar with listening to lies, Satan's craftiness has often kept us from realizing that we have started believing them or that they are even lies (or half-truths) at all.

I'll share some of my lies with you first to get you going. If I were to list some lies below, I'd write, "I'm unsuccessful. I'm unattractive, mainly because I'm overweight. I'm too much. I'm not enough. I'm too distracted. I'm a terrible mother. My husband probably doesn't even love me. I'm a failure." I could go on and on. Truthfully, even as

I wrote that list, a lie I thought of was that in sharing my list with you, I'd disqualify myself in your eyes from being able to be trusted by you. How dumb is that? Wouldn't Satan like us to keep hiding because he doesn't want to see me free or use my freedom to help you escape from where you are hiding? Today we end that!

What lies have you believed?

What truths have you twisted?

Look over that list of lies, think over the course of your life, and ask the Spirit to show you what might be a core lie you've believed. When I go over my lies, I've identified that my core lie is that I am insufficient. (The original title for this book was *Not Enough*, and I was going to have you cross out the "Not" on the cover when you finished reading the book.) My core lie has relatively stayed with the same message of not enough. You might be different. Your core lie might evolve with time or even completely change in messaging. That's another way Satan is crafty—he has a different attack plan for each of us. Identifying your core lie will help you be alert to the way Satan prowls after you.

What is your core lie?
If you need help, this is a great time to ask a trusted friend. Share your other list with them and see if they can help you identify it.

I'm sure now that you can see how Satan has used this core lie to attack you again and again. Because he is so crafty, he has tried different ways to communicate this lie to you. And our response to this lie isn't so different from Adam's and Eve's—we cover up and hide. I also want you to identify how you have covered up or hidden. Ask the Holy Spirit to reveal that to you. Write down if you sense Him leading you to a particular answer. This isn't a test that requires the right or perfect answer; this is an opportunity to become aware so you can have a better relationship with your Father.

"Where are you?"
Identify how you cover up your lies or hide from God.

The final question I have for you is the last one God asked Adam and Eve: "Who told you that . . . ?" Review your list of lies and try hard to identify the lies you believe and where you might hear those lies. For example, in processing my list of lies, I can see that a prevalent response would be social media. Satan can have a field day there with me. Satan whispers lies to me as I let my thumb lead me through the endless minefield of Instagram.

"Who told you that . . . ?"
Identify as many sources as you can. If possible, identify how each source communicates a lie to you.

Big hugs and fist bumps for your work so far. I know it wasn't easy! I have some good news for you. After Adam and Eve came out of hiding, God did something significant after He did something hard. First, there were consequences. They had sinned against God, so there had to be a consequence. When my kids do something wrong, I wouldn't be a loving parent if I didn't teach them by giving consequences. *But God.* He didn't leave the first couple disgraced in their shame, for He is always about redemption.

Genesis 3:21 shows the first blood sacrifice to cover man's sin: "The LORD God made for Adam and his wife garments of skin and clothed them." He could have left them in their sewn-together fig leaves. In the same way the first sacrifice had to be made to cover up the shame of Adam and Eve, the Father sent His Son, Jesus, to cover up our shame. Like Adam and Eve, we often try to cover up or hide. *But God can* provide a way out of hiding and an actual covering for our shame—the blood of Jesus.

Sometimes my brain struggles to understand how one man's blood can cover all my sins. I mean, I definitely like the idea of it, but I struggle with how it's possible. I find great comfort in verses like Hebrews 11:1: "Now faith is the assurance of things hoped for, the conviction of things not seen." You don't have to understand everything; that's where faith comes in. (And it's not just any man's blood. It's the blood of the perfectly innocent, perfectly capable Son of God.)

We all put our faith in something. Every single one of us. Most people who doubt that Jesus' blood could cover their sins don't doubt that Jesus lived on this earth and did what the Bible says He did. There is far too much historical evidence for His life. The only thing that keeps them from believing the validity of His sacrifice for them is faith. (We don't have space to dive into that here, but I highly recommend Lee Strobel's *The Case for Christ* and *The Case for Faith* to answer some of those "how" or faith questions.[2])

We've already read John 10:10 and learned that "the thief [Satan] comes only to steal and kill and destroy." But we didn't finish that verse. After Jesus exposed Satan's purpose, He was quick to reveal His own purposes: "I [Jesus] came that they may have life and have it abundantly." Satan has always been about destroying us, just as he attempted with Eve. *But God.* Friend, Jesus said that He came not so that you'd have a chance at life but so that you'd have *abundant* life. If you feel stuck simply surviving your days or circumstances, like you are spinning on a hamster wheel, I can assure you that Jesus wants more for you. He calls us to abundance, and I fully believe we will find that as we continue to work through these pages. On our own, we can't, *but God can!*

Eating from the Tree of Knowledge of Good and Evil was supposed to bring death to Adam and Eve. In a way, it did. The intimacy with God and freedom they had known in the garden were dead. *But God.* He made a sacrifice that restored them to a relationship with Him, allowing them to come out of hiding and break free of shame.

You have the same opportunity. He calls you to live abundantly. Would you say you are living abundantly now? Below are some synonyms for *abundantly* from the *Merriam-Webster Thesaurus*. See if these words apply to your life:

abounding	*overflowing*
ample	*plentiful*
blooming	*profuse*
extra	*rich*[3]
generous	

Don't read these words in regard to your possessions but to the measure of which you are experiencing life. Still not sure? After I look at synonyms, I sometimes explore antonyms to see if those feel more accurate. Do you relate more to these antonyms of *abundant*?

inadequate   *skimpy*
insufficient   *small*
lacking   *unfruitful*
meager   *unproductive*[4]
minimal

God is calling you to stop listening to the lies and receive Him so you can live an abundant life. It's possible!

I know you aren't there yet, but I hope you already have greater confidence to yell at Satan the same way Trevor yelled at his sister, "*Liiiiiiaaaarrrr! You're lying!*" These lies will no longer hold power over you because you are choosing to live abundantly instead.

Pray

Father, help me become more aware of the lies I've believed. Spirit, give me discernment as I go about my days to know where, when, and how I'm hiding. Reveal who or what is lying to me. I don't want to listen to or believe these lies anymore. Give me freedom from them! Thank You for sending Jesus to be my sacrifice and covering. I confess that at times I struggle to understand this sacrifice, but help my unbelief! Help me to trust in You more, Jesus—grow my belief and faith more and more. And help me to live abundantly, not the facade of abundance I might have grown accustomed to, but the true, abundant living You promised is possible.

Process

1. If you haven't already, go back and process what lies you believe and your core lie. How has believing these lies affected your life?

2. You identified who told you lies and where you've been hiding. How can you set up better boundaries to protect yourself from these things happening in the future? (If you feel stuck on this, ask the Spirit to show you, and you can also ask a trusted friend to help you figure out a solution.)

3. When you read the synonyms and antonyms for *abundant*, which list did you feel that your life most represented? How so? How does acknowledging that make you feel?

4. Define what abundant life for you might look and feel like. Identify some baby steps you could take right now to begin living abundantly.

Hearers & Doers Challenge

Today, set up one of your solutions for question 2 above.

For example, I shared that social media is a big struggle of mine. A solution for me with social media that has dramatically helped is choosing to celebrate with others and also unfollowing/muting those who bring me down. You have power, and you can unfollow anyone causing the lies to come up for you (or a "nicer" approach might be just to hide them from your newsfeed if you don't want to unfollow them). In addition, I've found it to be wildly helpful to cheer others on. When I stop mindlessly scrolling and instead heart/like every post I see and leave comments, I find that it's hard to hear lies when I'm busy loving others.

3

WHAT IS HOLDING YOU BACK?

If you can't fly then run, if you can't run then walk, if you can't walk
then crawl, but whatever you do you have to keep moving forward.
Martin Luther King Jr.

The first time I spoke in front of others was halfway through my junior year of high school, and I'd been a Christian for all of six months. I was totally and completely obsessed with Jesus. He had radically changed my life, and I could not get enough of Him or His Word. The chaplain at our school asked me if I'd be willing to share my testimony and a short message at a special all-girls chapel. I was terrified, but again, I was in the honeymoon phase of my relationship with Jesus and said yes before I realized what I was saying yes to. I prayed a lot and prepped just as much, and the day finally came. I remember walking into the room and seeing more than one hundred high school girls. As I looked into their eyes, fear hit me.

All of a sudden, all these lies came flooding into my mind: *Who do you think you are leading chapel? Don't you know that all these girls know who you were just six months ago? Do you think they will really believe you've changed? They know too much. And who do you think you are teaching the Bible? You just started reading it six months ago!* I was too young in my faith to know about lies or how to fight them, but I knew Jesus. I took a deep breath, prayed, and opened my mouth. I don't remember much about what I said, but I remember two things: lives were changed that day, and I stopped breathing.

Yes, God did His thing despite me. When I say I stopped breathing, I'm not kidding. I didn't pass out or hyperventilate, but I forgot to breathe, and then I couldn't remember how to breathe; it was like I was gasping for breath between sentences. I allowed fear to grip me. What is significant about this moment is that it would plague me for the next few years. I didn't know then that my wild passion for God's Word and absolute obsession with Him would prepare me to teach thousands of women one day. What I also didn't know then but do now is that Satan also knew what God was up to, and he tried his hardest to take me out. I was asked many times over the next couple of years to speak and teach, and every single time it would happen again—God would do something special, but I would forget how to breathe. It got so bad that even making announcements at my sorority would be a challenge because, for those two minutes, I would forget how to breathe.

One day this all changed. I was a freshman at Texas A&M, and we had a prayer night at the student center. We were in one of those huge ballrooms that could hold all three hundred of us, but the room was totally cleared out and pared down. They encouraged us to spread out, then guided us through a special prayer time. I've never heard the voice of God audibly, but I do pay attention to the impressions I believe the Spirit makes in me. And that night, I heard God clearer than I'd ever heard Him before. It was undeniably Him. I remember I knelt down with my face planted on that musty wood floor so my body could express what my heart felt. I wanted to live surrendered to God and the life He had for me. I can't remember what I was praying specifically, only that I was asking God to take away this fear of speaking because I knew He was calling me to do this more and more. I sensed the Lord saying, "Never say no to me again out of fear." This was specifically regarding teaching and leading because I couldn't breathe when I was in front of people. Because I was afraid, I had been running away from what I knew God was leading me to do. What I didn't know is that those words would become the guiding factor that would lead me these past two and a half decades since that moment.

Fear comes in many forms for me: fear of failure, success, looking like a fool, and rejection. It's ridiculous how long I could go on. Fear is the primary thing that holds me back. But other things—feelings, situations, and people—have held me back too. Sometimes I've let being a woman hold me back, or being a mother, not having enough money, or not being included or popular enough. It's essential for us to acknowledge what is holding us back from following God to live the life He has called us to. Think about your context and your life. In what ways are you being held back from living your life freely?

What is holding you back?

Spend less than a minute on this question. Jot down whatever comes to mind. We will process it later; this is just an initial brain and heart dump. Fear is my biggie, but I shared other things too. What are some of the things that are holding you back?

As women we often feel like this is just how it is, and there's not much we can do about it. However, friend, I want you to hear that you are not a prisoner to the parts of your life that aren't abundant.

About five years ago, a friend invited me and eight other women to a weekend of rest. She planned unique moments to be refreshed by the Lord and renewed in our purpose, which was perfect because I came in exhausted. For months I had been telling my husband, Chris, "I feel like I have so many spinning plates! I'm overwhelmed, but I don't know what to do." I was not living abundantly and desperately needed this retreat.

Every expectation was exceeded, each detail curated to make us feel delighted in by God the Father. Each meal was served on stunningly set tables—some in a dining room, some picnic style, and one in a field at night by candlelight. This attention to detail made us feel so special. On the final day of the retreat, when I was sitting in a rocking chair on the porch watching the most beautiful Texas sunrise, I sensed the Lord again, just like I had on that musty wood floor years ago: "Lay your plates down. Stop spinning them and set the table." I immediately realized I felt like I had to have spinning plates; I had to feel busy and overwhelmed because that was the season of life I was in. (Lie.) I was not a prisoner of my circumstances; I had the agency to make changes. So I listed all my spinning plates, every single one. I started with myself: my walk with Jesus, things I enjoy, my health, and so on. Next I went to relationships: my husband, kids, extended family, friends, neighbors. Then the roles I play or things I do: writer, speaker, coach and consultant, house cleaner, cook, volunteer. It wasn't until I saw all the plates that I realized why I felt overwhelmed. It was a lot!

After I laid down all my plates, I felt relieved and overwhelmed. A passage that is glaringly obvious when looking at all those spinning plates is one that we first looked at in my opening letter, Matthew 11:28–30: "Come to me, all who labor and are heavy laden, and I will give you rest. Take my yoke upon you, and learn from me, for I am gentle and lowly in heart, and you will find rest for your souls. For my yoke is easy, and my burden is light."

Nothing about my spinning plates felt easy or light, or as *The Message* paraphrases it, let me "live freely and lightly." I was overwhelmed by the hard, heavy, and busy. I continued rocking back and forth on that porch and waited. That's when the Lord showed me that I could take inventory now that I could finally see all my plates laid out:

- I could identify the plates that, while beautiful, didn't fit in my life or on my table anymore.
- I could identify the "broken" plates and see that it was time to part with them finally.
- I could see the plates I treasured and needed to better care for.
- I could see the plates that were good to have but weren't my faves, so they didn't need to come out as often and might need to be given away soon.

At each meal I'd been to, I had seen that not every plate belonged at every table. Those tables were breathtaking and cultivated a different experience because they were specifically curated. All that wasn't needed had been removed. So I went through my plates, one by one, and marked them. You can probably guess what I will ask you to do next, right?

Now it's your turn. Write on the plates provided each of your things (spinning plates).

Using the above examples I shared, go through the same categories and place each thing on a plate: personal life, relationships, roles, and whatever else comes to mind.

Go back to your plates and begin to reset your table. Mark the ones
that need to go, the ones that need to be treated more special, and
so on. Some plates you won't know how to mark—ask the Holy
Spirit what's best for you.

Congrats on completing that activity. I encourage you to continue
taking those plates to the Father to get His insight. Actively participate
in your life—that's how you take control of it. You might not be able
to change some plates, but you can adjust what table they go on or
how often they are used.

Now I want us to look at one of my favorite women in the Bible:
Tamar. A common thing said about her is that she was a shady lady,
but God used her anyway. I had always assumed that's how her story
went. A few years ago, I studied Genesis, and I was shocked when
we got to Tamar's life. I'll be honest: I actually threw my Bible study
across the room because I was so mad at what I'd read. Her incredibly
tragic-turned-powerful story is found in Genesis 38, tucked right in
the middle of the life of Joseph (the one with the colorful coat).

Tamar's story starts with Judah, Joseph's big brother, setting up
a marriage for his oldest son, Er, to Tamar. As it turned out, Er was
"wicked in the sight of the LORD, and the LORD put him to death"
(38:7). So then, as was customary in that day, Judah gave his next son,
Onan, to "perform the duty of a brother-in-law to her, and raise up offspring" for his brother (v. 8). (Yes, that means exactly what you think
it does.) But because Onan didn't like that the offspring wouldn't be
his, every time he "went in to his brother's wife he would waste the
semen on the ground, so as not to give offspring to his brother. And
what he did was wicked in the sight of the LORD, and he put him to
death also" (vv. 9–10).

This poor woman! In those days, women had little to no rights
(closer to no rights). They were the property of their fathers first, and

that ownership was passed to their husbands. Tamar had been put into a marriage with a man who was so wicked that God chose to kill him. I can only begin to fathom what that level of wickedness must have been like for Tamar to endure. Then she was thrust into another marriage, which ended up being an unpleasant sexual relationship with her deceased wicked husband's brother. (I know this sounds like a terrible soap opera, but it was Tamar's life.) This brother turned out to be just as wicked as his brother and also really, really selfish. He had no problem sleeping with Tamar and taking advantage of her physically, so much so that he was obviously pleasured, but he wouldn't allow her to have the one thing that could bring her worth: a child. So, again the man in her life was so wicked, the Lord put him to death. Part of me wants to filter Tamar's story, but this was her reality. Feel how truly horrible it was for her. Sadly, the story just gets worse.

Judah had one more son, Shelah, but he told Tamar to return home and remain a widow until Shelah grew up. So she went home and waited. Again, we don't know exactly how much time passed here or what those years would have been like. We know that she was still living like a widow, and we also learn that Judah, her father-in-law, had lost his wife. Tamar learned that Judah would be coming to town, and she must have assumed or heard that Shelah, the one she was told to wait for, would be with him. So she removed her widow's clothing and went to check things out. So as not to be noticed, she covered her face with a veil. And what she saw would have likely shocked her and retriggered all the trauma. While she had been waiting as a widow, Shelah had, in fact, grown up but had never been given to her in marriage.

This is where the story goes from detestable to infuriating. While Judah had ignored her all this time, he noticed her that day. However, he didn't recognize her since the veil covered her face. He assumed she was a prostitute and turned to her and said, "Come, let me come in to you" (v. 16). (This is where I had my hands gripped on the edges of my

Bible study, trying not to throw it.) So they discussed the terms of the arrangement. This part is confusing because we simply can't fathom this scenario. But remember, women had no rights. They were property. And Tamar had been married to two men who were so wicked that God had put them to death. She'd endured so much, and now her father-in-law offered to give her a goat in exchange for sex. However, he didn't have the goat with him, so he gave her his signet, cord, and staff as collateral until payment could be made. This is where Tamar always gets the bad rap. I'd always been taught that she was a prostitute. But that is not true—she was a woman who had been victimized and abandoned. She showed great strength that day by taking matters into her own hands; she was an active participant in her life when she could have shrunk away as a victim.

Remember, Judah, not Tamar, initiated this sexual encounter. Don't forget that Judah, not Tamar, held all the power and rights. The shock must have flushed over her as she was surely triggered by all the trauma and deceit she'd known at the hand of this family. She wasn't a deceiver; she was the one who had been deceived. She had done nothing, not a single thing wrong; this was all the fault of Judah and his boys. Judah was the one who thought Tamar was a prostitute, and he showed that he clearly had no problem sleeping with prostitutes. (Based on how this went, we can assume this wasn't his first time hiring a prostitute, but we don't know for sure.) It wasn't Tamar's first time being put in an uncomfortable situation where culture didn't allow her a way out. I told you this is an infuriating story!

The story gets even more twisted. Tamar got pregnant, and yes, the daddy was Judah, her father-in-law. Next we learn that Judah had sent the goat to pay the "prostitute," but there wasn't a prostitute to be found, and people said there never had been (further proving Tamar was not a prostitute). Three months later, Judah found out that his daughter-in-law was now pregnant. Judah's reaction? "Let her be burned" (38:24). (This is when I threw my study, not my Bible, across the room. I was livid for Tamar. Sickened over all that she had endured.) But Tamar handled the situation with so much dignity. She sent the proof to Judah—his signet, cord, and staff—saying the items belonged to the baby's father. Wouldn't you have loved to see Judah's face as he realized who those items belonged to?

While Christian society has often preached that Tamar seduced and tempted Judah, we can see this story through a more transparent lens now. I hope that we can also view her as Judah did. In verse 26, Judah truthfully proclaimed, "She is more righteous than I, since I did not give her to my son Shelah."

I understand this is an extreme example. I mean, weren't we just scribbling words on china plates? But I wanted to tell you a story of a biblical woman we could relate to. Tamar shows us that we all have things (plates) we can't control. You might have a diagnosis that has rocked your world. You might have a marriage that isn't as wicked as Tamar's but is less than satisfying. Your church might have burned you. You might have very challenging children. We all have plates we can't get rid of; we are stuck with them. We also all have plates we feel stuck with but could do something about; we just haven't yet.

Tamar's story should give you hope. She had every excuse to quit, and she could have quit and none of us would have blamed her. She wouldn't have such a bad reputation if she had quit, because people wouldn't wrongly have assumed things for hundreds of years. Likewise, you probably have things in your life that others would understand you giving up on. Even if you do keep spinning all the plates, people would understand because that's what we do, right? *But God* has something different for you. You must identify what's been holding you back and set down your spinning plates. And when you surrender this thing to the Father, He can do wonders with your life!

We learn that Tamar wasn't shady; she was strong! When life had betrayed her, she didn't quit and wait for things to work out. Even in the midst of trauma, she knew she couldn't be passive if she was going to live abundantly. Many Christian teachers have labeled Tamar one of the bad girls of the Bible. Let's not forget, though, that Judah declared her to be "more righteous." The redemption gets sweeter, because the next time we read about Tamar is in Matthew 1:3, in the genealogy of Jesus. Yes, Tamar was the great-great-great-great- (times a lot) grandmother of Jesus. *But God could* come to earth as a descendant of a woman who had been betrayed, victimized, traumatized, abandoned, and wrongly accused.

What kind of table might God be able to set for you if you lay down your plates? The things holding you back don't have to anymore; you can find freedom and hope in Jesus because He is more than able.

Father, I confess that I've been held back by [share what you wrote earlier]. I am asking that You would free me from this! I am laying down all these plates. They overwhelm me, so continue to show me which plates to let go of. There are some I really don't want to let go of, and there are some that I don't know how I can let go of. Show me also which ones I need to prioritize more and which ones need less of my focus. And finally, would You give me strong discernment and clarity when and if I add any new plates? Give me the courage of Tamar to be an active participant in my life!

1. For the thing(s) holding you back, see if you can find any verses to meditate on or memorize. For example, since fear is

my biggie, I would use Joshua 1:9, "Have I not commanded you? Be strong and courageous. Do not be frightened, and do not be dismayed, for the LORD your God is with you wherever you go."

2. What spinning plates would be the hardest to let go of? Why is it hard? Go an extra step: reflect on each of those plates, ask God how to let go of them, and record any answers you sense Him leading you to.
3. What are your thoughts about Tamar's story?
4. How do you need to be more courageous and proactive with your life?

Hearers & Doers Challenge

Who are some friends or mentors you could trust to review your plates? Invite them to give their feedback. Ask them if you are missing any. Let them know what you are sensing you should do about them—which ones need to go, which ones need more of you, which ones need less of you, and which ones might you need to add. Ask them what they think.

> **NOTE:** Just because you ask them does not mean you need to do what they say. You always need to trust the Spirit in you first and most. But community is a valuable thing the Lord has given us in living freely and lightly.

(4)

THINK DIFFERENTLY

> We can choose courage or we can choose comfort,
> but we can't have both. Not at the same time.
> Brené Brown, *Rising Strong: The Reckoning. The Rumble. The Revolution.*

Have you ever reorganized something just for it to end up a disaster again? That's me with my closet every single month. Chris was super excited the house we moved into a couple of years ago had two separate closets, because he is now free from my stack of clothes on the floor. Men don't understand that sometimes you need to try on approximately 498 outfits to pick the final one. The problem, though, isn't in my trying on so many options; it's that I don't take the time to hang them back up. (Does anyone else have a stack of perfectly clean clothes begging to go back on the hanger?) Inevitably, after a few weeks, even I will tire of the pile and will organize it. Every item will get hung up in absolutely perfect, color-coded order. I then vow not to let my closet get crazy again because I love the feeling of having it clean. Well, you can guess what happens the next month—rinse and repeat. I never change my thinking or make a plan to ensure that my clothes stay off the floor. Good intentions get me through week one, but I cave to old habits by week two.

Friend, already you've done a lot of work. I'm praying you feel hope starting to spring up that things will actually be different this time—not like my closet each month. We are just starting—we've addressed failures and lies and have put our tables in order. Now I want to teach you a skill that will make what you've learned and what you are still to process stick: learning to think differently.

A popular verse that we've taken out of context for far too long is "Above all else, guard your heart, for everything you do flows from it" (Proverbs 4:23 NIV). I became a Christian at sixteen, and strict boundaries for dating were all the rage, thanks in large part to the bestselling book *I Kissed Dating Goodbye*.[1] I was a prime target for teachings like this, and guarding your heart was central. It has been more than two decades since I read the book, but the following are my takeaways. The author, Joshua Harris, has since recanted what he said in the book and requested it no longer be published.

Harris has shared that he got caught up in the culture, not realizing that decades later people would still be recovering from how truth got twisted. The book was adamant that dating was wrong and courting was the way to go—courting being a very guarded relationship with someone with the intention of marriage. There was also very strong teaching on modesty. I believe this message was well-intentioned in encouraging women to be modest so as to help their brothers out and not tempt them. But decades later, we see the shame it poured on to women and how they see their bodies. Such teaching has also placed shame on men, causing them to hide sexual addiction or strongholds. The primary push of the book: no physical contact until marriage. While Christian culture had long advocated for no sex before marriage, Harris added to that by encouraging not even kissing until marriage. (This book is not the space to debate this; truthfully, none of us really knows what's best.) All this teaching sprang from one man's opinion on one out-of-context verse, likely supported by other out-of-context verses, and Christians ate it up, buying hundreds of thousands of books on these topics.

I hadn't exactly been the poster child for purity culture before I started following Jesus. So, as someone who is prone to "should-y" thinking, I dove deep into these teachings that I felt I should live out. I didn't have enough context of the Bible because I had just started reading it, so I didn't know any better. When a spiritual leader said, "Guard your heart," it was always in the context of relationships. I believed them. In their defense, I think they believed themselves. It wasn't that what they said was intentionally bad, but it wasn't a biblical truth, at least not as they were teaching it. As someone who had let others, especially boys, into my heart, I created a new mantra: "Guard your heart."

The problem is that the context of Proverbs 4 is a father speaking to his son. Before verse 23, the father instructed the son to pay attention to all the wisdom he was sharing and put it in his heart. So when he told his son to guard his heart, he wasn't telling him to guard his heart against falling for the wrong girl. He was saying to protect the good that is within because that's where life comes from. Everything one does springs from what is in the heart. The father continued to caution his son about being careful with his mouth and not to let anything corrupt come from it. He told him to keep his eyes fixed straight ahead. Then he said, "Give careful thought to the paths for your feet and be steadfast in all your ways" (4:26 NIV). We live and walk in wisdom when we protect our hearts and are careful with our thoughts.

The self-help culture, even Christian self-help, can have a field day teaching mind-over-matter mentalities. As a life coach, I'm not opposed to those teachings; there is definite validity to many of those principles.

But through the power of the Holy Spirit within, the believer has something greater than mind over matter. "For though we live in the world, we do not wage war as the world does. The weapons we fight with are not the weapons of the world. On the contrary, they have divine power to demolish strongholds. We demolish arguments and every pretension that sets itself up against the knowledge of God, and we take captive every thought to make it obedient to Christ" (2 Corinthians 10:3–5 NIV). There's so much hope in this passage for us. Your best option isn't to fake it till you make it, nor is it mind-over-matter mentalities. God tells us that even though we are in the world and have access to these teachings, we have to fight differently. How do we fight? We take every thought captive. My hope is that as you continue through this chapter, you will learn how to do that. Remember, though, as with so much you'll learn in these pages, this takes practice. Two steps forward, one step back. Progress, not perfection.

Recently I went to see my counselor, Ruth. She gave me a daunting assignment: brainstorm every terrible thought I have had about myself, that I believed others thought about me, that I thought about others, that I thought about God, and that I believed God thought about me, as well as every bad thought I had about my place or purpose in this world. It was quite a daunting session. However, it was, sadly, very easy to do. Why are we so good at recalling bad things about ourselves while struggling to think of the good? The negative thoughts from each category flew off my tongue and onto the giant sheets she had stuck on the walls.

While I felt safe with Ruth, I felt exposed to share thoughts I'd never spoken out loud—not with my husband, closest friends, or even the Lord. I sat on her couch, just as I invited you onto mine when we first started this journey together. She stood before me with a giant paper taped to her wall and a marker in her hand. Her eyes held patience, security, and grace. I began to feel comfortable enough to share things I'd thought about myself. I saw her write those thoughts on the paper, and seeing them made me feel—honestly, it's hard to verbalize how it made me feel. I felt more vulnerable than I'd ever been in my entire life. I had never acknowledged many of those thoughts, and now they felt like a giant billboard on her office door. Yet there was freedom in the release. The facade was gone. No longer was I pretending that I didn't think or feel those things. While the vulnerability of it felt a little terrifying, I felt freedom in being exposed along with great hope of what would come of this.

You can probably guess what I will ask you to do now. Yes, I want you to do the same thing. Use the space below to list the thoughts you might have. Remember, don't overthink this; there's no judgment here. Let's be honest with ourselves. As Ruth said, with her unpretentious smile and a spark in her eyes, "Let's get really dark here!" Friend, you are free to be honest and safe to be vulnerable. I didn't want to do it either. I felt too exposed. I wanted to guard my heart by not letting anyone see what was in it, but I knew the best way to guard my heart was to let out the thoughts that didn't bring life. So out flowed all those thoughts. I hope you have the same freedom. Remember, the thoughts don't have to be rational or even true; they are just thoughts you've had.

List every terrible thought you have had about yourself.

List every terrible thought you have believed others thought about you.

List every terrible thought you have thought about others.

List every terrible thought you have thought about God.

List every terrible thought you have believed God thought about you.

And finally, list every terrible thought you've had about your place or purpose in this world.

Oh my goodness! I know how vulnerable that work is. You will not regret this, I promise! I'm also really excited for you because while recording all of that is vulnerable, it's also freeing. I thought I would have only regret after going really dark, as Ruth had asked, by sharing all my thoughts. But what I felt was free and light. Simply putting those thoughts out there took them off of myself.

You might know this from personal experience, or maybe you've seen it in a show or a movie, but when pregnant in your final trimester, it's a workout to do basic things like roll over in bed or get off the ground. I remember having instant relief shortly after delivering my first daughter. All of a sudden I felt like there wasn't an entire human inside of me. That's how I felt this day; I didn't even realize how heavy those thoughts had been to carry around. However, the minute I let them out, I felt instant relief.

When we were done, Ruth peeled the paper with my thoughts off the wall, rolled them up, and said, "Hang these up somewhere. Then look at them and ask God what happened in your life that would have caused you to think these thoughts. One by one, go through each thought, and next week we will talk about what you discover." This felt like the equivalent of me asking you to snap a picture of your answers to the prompts and post them on social media. Um, no thanks, hard pass. Right?

So I took that roll of paper and drove home. Instead of processing through my thoughts, I immediately shoved them into the back of my closet. I didn't want anyone to see that list! I didn't want to acknowledge most of those things again, much less hang them up for anyone to see. So I kept them rolled up and hidden in my closet until the day before my next session. I knew I needed to do my homework, so I pulled out that paper containing all my darkest thoughts. Then, one by one, I gave each thought its space and tried to think about what had happened that caused me to think that thought about myself, others, or God. This wasn't easy; many of them were utterly heartbreaking. I hadn't ever slowed down to think through why I thought so many of the thoughts I had. I was so busy trying not to think of them that I hadn't given them space to learn why they were there.

> Go back to each prompt and each thought you listed, and ask yourself, *What might have caused me to think this?*

I found that I needed to block off some time to think through the reasons for my thoughts. This might be a page you earmark and come back to. But please be intentional to return to it; put it on your calendar. If you can take some time now, do it. Ponder what could have contributed to each thought. I am the queen of justifying all things; please fight to not be the same way.

At my next counseling session, I took my list to Ruth and we went through each thought and what experiences might have caused or contributed to believing that thought. What's interesting about thoughts we've had for a long time is that we normalize them. We don't see how we are off because we've always viewed ourselves, others, or God that way. I would share a thought, and then I would share the two or three examples that happened in my life to affirm the thought as true. Again and again, Ruth would say, "Wow! I can see now why you would think that!"

I was shocked! How? How could she see that? How could she justify those thoughts? And then she taught me the lesson that I'm still learning: *We can validate our thoughts without condoning the behavior that comes from believing those thoughts.* If I had to look at your list, I feel confident I could say the same to you as Ruth said to me. Most of us have an easy time validating others while shaming ourselves.

I struggle with validating myself because I "should" know better (my counselor agrees that I have very "should-y" thinking). Hearing her say again and again, "Wow! I can see why you would think that," felt awkward. Even though many of the thoughts were ridiculous, once they were paired with the reason for believing them, they made sense. I had to go through each thought that week and write over it, "I can see how you would think this." One by one, I validated each thought. I didn't condone behavior that might have come from my thoughts; I simply validated them.

Your turn! Go through each thought and say or write, "I can see how you would think that."

Don't rush past this activity. Give each thought time. Don't write or say, "I can see how you would think that" until you really can see it. (Tip: If you write on top of what you said before, it helps cover it up too!)

Doing this has changed how I see myself, others, and God. The shame deep within me was slowly peeled back one layer at a time. It wasn't lip service or simply checking a box. To slow down and identify why I believed each of those thoughts was freeing. Proclaiming grace and validation over those thoughts has drastically changed me. I don't carry shame or guilt for many of these thoughts; instead, I carry an understanding. I truly can see why I would think those things. It makes sense. (I will always hear those two phrases in Ruth's comforting Kenyan accent.)

We already know we've been told many lies in our lives, and "failures" and setbacks haven't helped as we've wanted to live a "but God can" life. However, we have to clear our heads and begin thinking differently if we want to see God do what only He can do. To find what is true, we are about to begin to work through the primary negative thoughts and feelings we've identified. Invite the Father to speak new truths to your old thoughts. Go through each thought above and ask God to show you what is true.

Even though it makes sense that you would think something based on what has happened, let's start to correct those thoughts now. I've learned that validation is essential to the healing process. Validating why you would think something doesn't excuse behavior and isn't being soft; it's loving yourself like the Father loves you. However, just because we can see why we would think something doesn't mean we should continue to think that way. Now that we've identified them, it's time to take our thoughts captive and begin correcting them.

Easier said than done, right? Here's a very common example: most women think they're unattractive. The reasons are unlimited:

fad diet culture, magazine covers, what others have said, and so on. We can validate those thoughts and say, "I can see why you would think that because of all those reasons." But then we can change our thoughts by saying, "God's Word says in Psalm 139 that I am fearfully and wonderfully made, and Genesis 1 says that I am made in God's image. If both of those things are true, then there's no chance I am ugly."

We must replace the lies we've believed with the truth we've been given by God. Then we can also bring in other truths. So using the above example, you can add all the ways you are beautiful. Maybe your eyes sparkle when you smile, you have the best laugh ever, your hair is movie-star gorgeous, or your sense of style is innately cool. This will feel uncomfortable because new ways of thinking always are, but speak what is true. Ask the Father to show you.

I am excited for you. Can you even imagine what's to come for you? If we really stopped seeing our "failures," believing lies, spinning plates, and listening to thoughts that aren't true, what in the world might God do? *But God can* do absolutely anything in your life. Keep going. I can't wait to see what He does!

Pray

Father, thank You for helping me to be vulnerable with myself and You. I feel so much shame for these thoughts. Thank You for helping me to see where they came from. Thank You for helping me see that there's a reason I've thought all of this for so long. I don't need to feel bad for that, but it's also not an excuse. And help me not to skip validating nor stay stuck validating. Teach me how to take my thoughts captive and think new thoughts. It feels so awkward; it feels so unworthy. Help me to believe what You say is true. Teach me to listen to Your Spirit, Lord.

Process

1. Have you thought "guard your heart" means protecting yourself in a guarded way in relationships? How do you interpret that verse now? What would it look like to guard your heart?
2. Were there any reasons that surprised you as you went through causes for thoughts? How so?
3. Which new thought means the most? Are there any you should hang up where you can see them often (like on your bathroom mirror, desk, above the sink, etc.)?
4. Are there any other ways you've learned to help take your thoughts captive?

Hearers & Doers Challenge

Your challenge for this chapter is to do the reflection questions here. If you haven't already done so, schedule an appointment to make it happen. Take the time to process each of those steps. If you feel stuck on some parts, invite someone you trust to provide insight.

5

GOD CAN MAKE A WAY

God can do nothing for me until I recognize the limits of what
is humanly possible, allowing Him to do the impossible.
Oswald Chambers, *My Utmost for His Highest*

Just before my oldest started kindergarten, I was feeling really off. For a couple of months, I chalked it up to having a baby, a toddler, and another going off to school for the first time. Having three girls within four years isn't for the faint of heart, so I expected to be exhausted. However, after a couple of months of this, I knew something wasn't right. I booked an appointment with my doctor. After listening to all my symptoms, he did a full physical and decided to run some tests to cover all the bases.

Two weeks later, I got the nurse's first call as I was walking up to the school to pick up Karis, my oldest, who had just turned six and started kindergarten a few weeks prior. I remember pushing both my littles, still groggy from their naps, with one hand, and holding the phone with the other. Moriah, our middle daughter, was three and a half (the half is always important at that age), and Chandler, our youngest daughter, had just turned one. The nurse said in her highest-pitched voice, riddled with nervousness, "Well, Mrs. Kiser, some of the tests came back abnormal, so we want to send you to get a few more tests. It's likely nothing, but we want to be thorough."

Some people overreact in situations like these, but I tend to underreact—it's half the reason I'd waited so long to go to the doctor. I thought nothing of it, went to get the tests, and really forgot about it until I got the next call. I was waiting in the carline to pick up Moriah from Mother's Day Out. Chandler was asleep in her car seat in the back, and I saw the doctor's number pop up on the screen and answered quickly. "Mrs. Kiser, well, unfortunately, those tests came back and are indicating [insert some medical terminology I can't remember because everything got fuzzy after this]. We need you to see [some specialty] oncologist." Again, I was fuzzy, so I'm not sure exactly how I responded, but I was pretty sure she said my next step was to go to an oncologist when I had fully expected her to say everything was normal and that all I needed was to drink more water, do actual yoga in my yoga pants, and sleep more.

"I'm sorry, oncologist? Do you think I have cancer?"

"Well, we don't know exactly what is going on, but we want you to see this doctor, and they will be able to run the next round of tests so we can find out." I grabbed a pen and scribbled the information on the back of a Chick-fil-A bag (because that's the only paper I had in my minivan).

A week later, I was in the oncologist's office, and they were starting a battery of tests to figure things out. It was at the next appointment that I finally started to worry about what was happening. Until this point, I really had chalked it all up to the stress of this stage of life. Thankfully, my best friend, Kelley, insisted on coming with me that day because I didn't remember anything as soon as the doctor said, "Mrs. Kiser, after looking at all of your tests, we believe you have either chronic myeloid leukemia or [some other rare blood disorder thing]." After I heard the word *leukemia*, I heard nothing else. What? How could this be? More tests would be ordered to confirm, and more waiting.

We did the tests, one after another, and then the wait began. Those weeks were a blur; I think it was two, maybe three. I remember choking back sobs as I watched my girls twirl around our house, which is always a nonstop dance party. I remember being in the shower, wishing I could scrub away whatever was growing in me, and feeling so completely helpless.

I also remember sitting at my dining room table and the Lord leading me to Isaiah 43. We looked at the beginning of the chapter when we talked about failures. Remember, verse 2 says, "When [not if] you pass through the waters . . . when [not if] you walk through fire. . . ." This verse resonated with me for sure. I was passing through waters and fire I had never known, and I have known many waters and fires. This one was different. The verses that really got me were verses 18–21: "Remember not the former things, nor consider the things of old. Behold, I am doing a new thing; now it springs forth, do you not perceive it? I will make a way in the wilderness and rivers in the desert . . . . for I give water in the wilderness, rivers in the desert, to give drink to my chosen people, the people whom I formed for myself that they might declare my praise."

I sat and stared at those verses over and over again. I felt so seen by the Father. I felt hope—not necessarily for healing but for possibility. The Bible isn't a Magic 8 Ball or my daily horoscope. I don't believe in the "name it and claim it" fads. But I do believe that God's Word tells us who He is, what He is capable of, and because of that, what is possible in our lives.

I learned that day that God was saying He was able to make a way in the wilderness and rivers in the desert. I don't know if you've ever been in a forest or someplace similar that is fully overgrown. I felt every bit like I was stuck in the middle of the wilderness. I was looking every which way and unsure of where to turn, what to do, or if I'd ever find my way out. God was saying in His Word that *He* was capable of making a way. I didn't need to grab a saw and slowly hack out a path, nor did I need to attempt crawling out. For one, my little saw couldn't possibly clear a path, and my body would have been covered in scratches, bruises, and countless bug bites. Instead, I only needed to trust that God, who created heaven and earth, would make a way where there seemed to be no way.

So when I find myself in the desert, I need to learn to trust God instead of trying to find a drink on my own. When I am parched and weary and blistered by the sun, God wouldn't just bring me a cup of water to quench my thirst. He wouldn't just bring me a well to allow me to pull up what water I needed. Nor would our Father bring me one river. Instead, He would bring rivers. Plural. How lavishly He is able to love us! We can't, *but God can*!

I'll be honest: I still struggle to receive and believe this. I constantly feel like the father in Mark who begged Jesus to heal his son if he could. To which Jesus replied, "'If you can'! All things are possible for one who believes" (9:23). With his sick son in his arms, the father replied honestly to Jesus, "I believe; help my unbelief!" (v. 24). I feel safe and seen when I read passages like this. Jesus healed the boy, "took him by the hand and lifted him up, and he arose" (v. 27). That's what Jesus did for me that day. I knew He could heal me, and I begged Him for that. But that day I also believed that even if He didn't heal me, even if the diagnosis was what the doctors thought it might be and I was looking at less than five years left with my family, I trusted that He could make a way in my wilderness and bring me rivers to nourish me as I walked through this desert. Sometimes He makes a way out, and other times He simply sustains us through.

We all have significant and seemingly insignificant things that we struggle to trust God for because our wilderness is so overgrown and our desert seems so stark. My primary motivation for sharing this message with you is responding to our culture's solutions to our mountains and wilderness. I am all for positivity and motivation—kind of a key character trait for a life and business coach. However, I am completely opposed to things that fall flat when pressed. Right now, especially for women, we are bombarded with "You can do this, girl!" mantras and motivations. This is true even within Christian culture—we've jumped on the girl-power movement.

The truth is that sometimes (or oftentimes) we don't have what it takes. The awareness of this isn't a lack of faith; it's the gospel message. We don't have to have what it takes. We can't, *but God can*! Letting this not just be your new mantra but a way you choose to live is audacious! Oh, friend, I hope you are ready to live audaciously. Let's be like the father, where we scoop up our mountain and go and say, "I believe; help my unbelief. I can't, *but God can*!"

The gospel, or good news, of Jesus is that we don't have what it takes. The pressure is off! In 2 Corinthians 12, we learn that Paul had a thorn in his flesh, and he had begged multiple times for God to take it away, and He hadn't. Can you relate? From what we know of Paul, it wasn't for a lack of faith that this thorn hadn't gone away. There are times when our mountains won't budge—the treatment didn't work, counseling didn't help, reconciliation was denied, unexpected expenses piled up, or the speed of life has worn you out. This is when the self-help mantras, even the Christian ones, begin to fall flat.

What do we do when the diagnosis is worse than we expected? What do we do when the marriage fails? What do we do when we fall back into the same temptations? What do we do when we can't stop losing our temper with our kids? What do we do when we keep zoning out and scrolling on our phones? What do we do when . . . ? Sometimes, actually, oftentimes, things don't work out as we'd hoped. This is where many of us begin to doubt God or at least doubt God's goodness. I used to be frustrated that Paul was so vague here. Many scholars have studied this, and there are many theories, but I don't think God wants us to know. I think He was intentionally vague because we can step into this story and let what Paul wrote next fit our situations.

A handful of Bible passages are absolute anchors for me, and 2 Corinthians 12:9–10 is one of them: "But he said to me, 'My grace is sufficient for you, for my power is made perfect in weakness.' Therefore I will boast all the more gladly of my weaknesses, so that the power of Christ may rest upon me. For the sake of Christ, then, I am content with weaknesses, insults, hardships, persecutions, and calamities. For when I am weak, then I am strong." While our culture would like us to think that we can do anything, Jesus came because we couldn't do it all. There is no shame in weakness. In fact, what this verse teaches us is that when we embrace our weaknesses, we get to experience the power of Christ! When you finally admit that you can't, you get to see that Jesus absolutely can.

Which leads me back to the doctor's office to get the results. I remember the nurse taking my blood pressure before the doctor came in, and she said, "That can't be right," after she took it a third time because it was so high. I looked her in the eye and said with a lighthearted smile, "I have three little girls, and I'm about to find out if I have leukemia or not. It's not going to go down until I see the doctor." I was finding out if God would lead me out of this wilderness or if He would ask me to trust that He would provide water in the desert. The doctor came in, my husband held one of my hands, and my other hand clenched my purse, which was filled with letters of encouragement and verses from some of my closest friends. Then, with disbelief, he said, "I don't know what happened, but it's nothing. All your tests are now completely normal." I was one of those rare cases the medical community struggles to explain and rarely is willing to call a miracle. In due diligence, I went to another doctor for a second opinion. This doctor looked at all my tests and results and confirmed they would've thought the same thing: likely leukemia. Then they ran more tests because it didn't make sense to them either. All came back clear—*but God can*!

I don't know what happened; I've never experienced anything like that before. Did I have leukemia and experience healing? That feels bold to claim but entirely possible and the only explanation I have that makes any sense. Were all those initial tests all false positives? It's unlikely for so many repeat tests to all be false positives. We will never know, but it is how I see the way God made for me in my wilderness. I couldn't, doctors couldn't, *but God* absolutely *can*, and this time He did!

What I do know is that season taught me Isaiah 43 in the most tangible way. I will never forget it, and I'll commit my life to helping you and countless other women know that it's possible for them too. We may not necessarily get our desired outcome, *but God can* either make a way or sustain us. Whatever it is, we can't, *but God can*! If He doesn't clear the path, we can trust that He is more than able and will provide water in our desert places.

I'm imagining the things you feel like you can't be or do—big and small—and I validate each of those feelings. I'm not going to pretend they aren't real. This book is not going to train you to fake it until you make it. We've done that, and it's exhausting and rarely works. Just as we aren't treating God like a genie in a bottle, we also aren't going to pretend like everything is fine. Instead, we are going to learn how to admit we can't so that we can experience a power we've never known. This power will either make a way where there seems to be no way or sustain us through whatever we are facing.

What are some seemingly small or slightly insignificant things in your life that feel like weaknesses?

This is the part most women struggle to acknowledge because they feel petty stating these things. Listen, this can be as small as "I struggle to keep my house clean" or "I can't stop gossiping with my coworkers." Nothing is too small here.

What are significant things in your life that feel like weaknesses?
This is where you can list the biggies—a failed marriage, diagnosis, parent wounds, addiction, and so on.

You aren't alone in this; I am with you. But even more, the Father is with you. He sees your weakness, and while He doesn't revel in it, He can step in and show off His power. You can't, *but God* totally *can*!

Go back and write "But God Can" on top of both of those lists you just made.

I hope you are starting to get and believe the *But God Can* concept. This mindset shift takes time. Remember, give yourself grace, just not too much. In the next chapter, we will go through a few of the circumstances we often find ourselves in and learn how to change our mindsets.

Pray

Father, thank You that I don't have to make a way because You will make one. Help me to have faith that You can do absolutely anything—a miracle to make a way out of the wilderness or to give sustaining water in the desert. Thank You for allowing me to be weak and that I don't have to do or be all with You. Help me to stop trying so hard and start trusting You instead. Father, help me to be open to shifting my mindset as I continue this book.

Process

1. Which of the weaknesses you listed affects your life the most right now?
2. Has there been a time, seemingly insignificant or monumental, when you've experienced a "but God can" moment or outcome? What was it?
3. What other verses or stories in the Bible encourage you to believe that God can do absolutely anything?
4. Does someone in your life need to hear this message too? Reach out to them and specifically encourage them in whatever they are facing. Remind them that Jesus has the opportunity to show them His power when they are weak, so they don't need to feel ashamed of that! (Bonus: Ask them to read through this book with you!)

Hearers & Doers Challenge

One of the things that was really helpful for me when I was going through that cancer scare was printing off the Isaiah 43 passage and posting it all over my house. I also sent it to all my friends and family and asked them to pray that passage over me. One of the ways to switch our mindset is to change what we are thinking about. This doesn't happen naturally. You have to train your mind, just like you'd have to train your body to run a marathon. I printed off the verse and posted it all the places in my house where I would spend time (not just in passing): on my bathroom mirror, by my kitchen sink, in my closet, above my washer and dryer, on my back door, and so on. When fear or weak thoughts would start to creep in, I'd say that verse and pray. It was always before me. What verse could you do the same with that resonates with you and your circumstances?

PART 2

LET GOD DO A NEW THING

When we first began together, I envisioned inviting you into my home. You sat on my couch, wrapped up in a plush blanket, and began sharing your story. While the couch has been cozy, the life coach in me can't let us stay comfortable. My friend, it's time to move forward.

I've told you about my Mamaw, but I haven't told you about my Papaw, her husband. We called him Boss-Boss because he was the boss at work and the boss at home. I loved him bossing me around and have missed it so much since he's been gone. One of the most sacred spaces was their kitchen table. They kept the fridge stocked with drinks and ice cream for us, likely so we'd always stay a little longer at the table. It worked—we would sit there for hours and have what my papaw called "big talk." He wasn't a small-talk man; he preferred to get down to it. He wanted to know everything happening in your life, especially the problems. He also wanted to find solutions or offer his perspective on each thing—hence the name Boss-Boss. He wasn't scared to hurt your feelings with the truth if it was what you needed to hear. He also wasn't afraid to make sure you knew he was proud of you or thought you were on the right track. Oh, I miss that table, his voice, and the mischievous sparkle in his eyes. I miss how he used to call me Boss-Boss Junior because I was just like him.

Since I'm Boss-Boss Junior, I'm inviting you to come off the couch and join me at the table so we can have our own "big talk." This table of ours will feel sacred and holy, and I'm begging that God would lead us on our way. I'm constantly asking the Lord to help me feel the weight of your burdens and the lightness of your joys. The juxtaposition of these two feelings is challenging to process, so I'm begging God to make these words life-changing and life-giving for you. I can't promise Blue Bell ice cream, but I can promise you'll be seen, heard, led, and loved by the Father. We've already laid down our spinning plates; all that's left is to simply come to the table. We can't do what's next on our own, *but God can*!

YOU FEEL EXHAUSTED, BUT GOD MAKES YOU STRONG

exhausted (adjective) / ig-ˈzȯ-stəd

1: completely or almost completely depleted of resources or
   contents

2: depleted of energy: extremely tired

synonyms: burnt-out, spent, weary, fatigued, wiped out[1]

The cancer scare wasn't the first medical thing I'd been through. I had seven surgeries in my senior year of high school and another three in my freshman year of college. To say I was "completely depleted" was an understatement. I was exhausted—physically, emotionally, mentally, and spiritually. I wanted—no, I needed—God to change things, and He wasn't doing that. It seemed as if things would never get better. This persistent health issue often led me to the hemorrhaging woman in Mark 5:25–34.

There we find Jesus on his way to healing the daughter of one of the synagogue rulers. A great crowd surrounded Jesus and His disciples as they journeyed, and all of a sudden Jesus stopped because He felt power go out from Him. He asked, "Who touched my garments?" (v. 30). The disciples found this an odd question because there were people all around Him. But as Jesus looked over the crowd, a woman stepped forward and, trembling, fell at his feet and told him what had happened.

This woman had endured a discharge of blood for twelve years. We are told in verse 26 that she "had suffered much under many physicians, and had spent all that she had, and was no better but rather grew worse." Twelve years. Think about where you were twelve years ago and imagine having the worst period of your life for all this time. Imagine your bank account being empty because you kept searching for a cure. And worse yet, for those twelve years, you were considered unclean, kept isolated from people, and unable even to enter the temple courts for women because of this affliction you couldn't get rid of.

While my health issues weren't to the extent of this woman's, I could see myself in these pages of Scripture. I was in awe of this woman. Even after twelve years of failed attempts at healing, she never stopped trying. She heard of Jesus and hoped again, believing that simply touching the edge of His clothes could heal her. How many doctors had she been to? How many times had she tried? And yet she still believed that maybe just a touch of Jesus' garments could be the thing to heal her.

And she was right. She reached out, and instantly she was healed. This was a miracle. So when Jesus stopped and asked who had touched Him, her heart must have been pounding. All this time, she'd been cast out socially, but now she'd just pushed through a crowd, essentially making everyone she'd been by unclean, including Jesus. Yet when Jesus asked, she came forward. She was afraid, surely exhausted, and told Him the truth.

Do you know what Jesus did? He told her, "Daughter, your faith has made you well; go in peace, and be healed of your disease" (v. 34). He called her "daughter." We've talked about names and identities in this book. This woman's old name would have been "outcast," but now Jesus called her "daughter"; that must have healed many wounds for her. She went from being alone to being in a family. He could have called her "sister" or "friend," but he chose "daughter." This is interesting because she may have been close to Jesus' age or older. (If she started her period around age twelve and the bleeding problem started then, she would be at least twenty-four. We know that Jesus started his public ministry around age thirty.) The word used for *daughter* here isn't a nickname for little girls; it's the same word used throughout the New Testament to indicate a biological daughter. It was as if Jesus was letting her know that she wasn't alone and that He was there to take care of her.

Let's look at 2 Corinthians 12:7–10 again in this context but this time in *The Message* paraphrase so you can hear it fresh:

> Because of the extravagance of those revelations, and so I wouldn't get a big head, I was given the gift of a handicap to keep me in constant touch with my limitations. Satan's angel did his best to get me down; what he in fact did was push me to my knees. No danger then of walking around high and mighty! At first I didn't think of it as a gift, and begged God to remove it. Three times I did that, and then he told me,
>
> My grace is enough; it's all you need.
> My strength comes into its own in your weakness.
>
> Once I heard that, I was glad to let it happen. I quit focusing on the handicap and began appreciating the gift. It was a case of Christ's strength moving in on my weakness. Now I take limitations in stride, and with good cheer, these limitations that cut me

down to size—abuse, accidents, opposition, bad breaks. I just let Christ take over! And so the weaker I get, the stronger I become.

What is exhausting you right now?

Don't negate it just because it seems insignificant or small; write it down. Write out the big and heavy things, the seemingly silly and mundane.

I'm not sure what is exhausting you now or what will exhaust you in the future. We all have things that tend to ebb and flow with each changing season. Two things I've learned from this passage give me hope in my exhaustion. First, Paul had something, too, and we learn that what made him weary literally brought him to his knees. He saw this as a good thing. While Satan wanted the thorn in Paul's flesh to take him out completely, God used it to draw him in. Now, Paul kept it real; he admitted that he did beg for God to change things. So I want to say, whatever is making you weary right now, it's okay to pray for God to change your circumstances. However, some circumstances might not change for reasons we might never know.

Second, Paul realized it was okay to be weary since Christ got to show off His strength when Paul was weak. I can't tell you how much hope this has brought me, and I trust it brings you hope too. Paul said that once he learned this, he stopped caring about what made him weak; instead, he began to appreciate his weakness. He saw that the weaker he got, the more he experienced Christ's strength.

Have you heard the verse "I can do all things . . ."? I'm sure you have—we love to use it at sporting events and in hard times. It's the banner we wave to proclaim that we can and will do anything. How we tend to take it out of context aligns with self-help mantras. While not bad, it's not exactly accurate. The context of this verse is that Paul was trying to reassure the Philippians that even though he had experienced persecution and imprisonment, he would be okay. He said, "I have learned in whatever situation I am to be content. I know how to be brought low, and I know how to abound. In any and every circumstance, I have learned the secret of facing plenty and hunger, abundance and need. I can do all things through him who strengthens me" (4:11–13). When Paul referenced being able to do all things, he didn't mean that he could literally do all things. He meant that he could do all the things God had for him because God would give him strength through it all. He also communicated that he could be content in whatever circumstances he found himself in.

I want to ensure that you hear this directly: you can't do everything.

I know, I know. How anti-feminist that statement is. But it's the most woman-empowering thing I can say to you, and I often say it to my girls. You can't do everything, nor can you be everything. Likely you are weary from all the trying. Instead, if you do what you are called to and are the woman God has called you to be while resting on Jesus to be your strength, you will feel more life than you've ever known. You will no longer be content with the hamster wheel or the mundane. Instead, you will be content in the place the Father sees best for you.

In looking at what makes you feel exhausted, is there anything you should stop doing or do differently? If so, write it below along with an action plan you can implement to eliminate what's exhausting you. If not, but if something is excessively exhausting that you can't stop, ask the Father to bring you strength.

Friend, I know you feel exhausted or overwhelmed by everything happening or not happening in your life. *But God can* make you strong. Remember that! You don't have to concede to a life of exhaustion just because that's how others say things are in this season. Let's stop trying so hard to be strong. Instead, let's be like the woman with the bleeding problem and reach out, trusting in God's power, not our own.

Pray

Father, I confess that I am exhausted; I am weary from [list things that are causing you to be or feel exhausted]. I don't want to live weary any longer. Instead, I want to learn how to find my strength in You. Lord, please help me not to try to push through the exhaustion or to put up fake mantras to pretend my circumstances will get better quickly. I believe Philippians 4:13, that I can do all the things that You call me to—the good, the bad, the hard, the easy—because I know You will give me just enough strength and oxygen for what I need. Help me boast in my weaknesses, like Paul, so I can know Your strength and power!

Process

1. Do you feel exhausted? By what? (Be as specific as possible.)
2. Has there been a time in the past when you've experienced God strengthening you? When? (Remembering how God has been our strength in the past helps us to trust that He can be our strength again.)
3. How can you let God strengthen you? What would that practically look like?
4. Which of the verses listed resonate with you the most? Why?

Hearers & Doers Challenge

Ideas and plans are great, but not if they never happen. You've processed some about what has contributed to exhaustion and also what could help you to receive God's strength.

First, pick one thing you will remove from your life right now that is draining you. This could be big (like a relationship) or small (like always doing the dishes—you can tag your husband, kids, or someone else to do them).

Second, pick one thing you will start doing this week that will contribute to you finding strength in the Father. This might be to listen to worship music on your commute to work or to wake up thirty minutes earlier to read your Bible or to start going to church weekly. What would strengthen you that you aren't consistently doing now? Put it on your calendar right now. Bonus if you also tell a friend about this and ask them to hold you accountable to follow through! You can do this; I believe in you!

7

YOU FEEL STAGNANT, BUT GOD HAS A PURPOSE FOR YOU

Stagnant (adjective) / ˈstag-nənt

1: not flowing in a current or stream; stale

2: not advancing or developing

synonyms: frozen, stuck, immovable, unbudging, motionless, static[1]

Many women feel stagnant, stuck in the life that keeps them busy but not truly fulfilled. They go through the motions but are going nowhere. We live anesthetized because choosing numbness is the easiest way to make it through this season. *Season*, that's how we qualify that this, too, shall pass. And it does, in fact, pass. But the next season brings more of the same; all that's changed are the circumstances.

Have you been there? Are you there now? You don't have to live stuck any longer. There is a better way for you! What if your life was described by these words instead: *loosened, freed, yielding, movable, flexible, alive, dynamic,* and *unbound* (all antonyms for *stagnant*)? For some of us, those words are terrifying too. We have a perceived sense of safety in being stuck; we are comfortable here even if we are unfulfilled.

One of the most popular verses in the Bible is Jeremiah 29:11: "For I know the plans I have for you, declares the LORD, plans for welfare and not for evil, to give you a future and a hope." Many claim this verse to assure themselves or others that everything will be okay. The problem with so many people taking this verse literally is that it wasn't a promise made to each of us but to the people of God when they were in exile. The Lord had sent Jeremiah to speak words of encouragement and truth to His people. He wanted them to know things would work out; they had reason to hope. However, they still had to wait more than seventy years until God brought them back to their promised land.

This verse and others read out of context should not be treated like a horoscope or a fortune cookie. Doing so will leave you asking questions like, "Why do bad things happen to good people?" "How could a loving God allow hard seasons in His people's lives?" God never promised us an easy life. Even as He declared a future and a hope over His people, that verse and the ones that follow were intended to remind them of who God is and how they could find comfort in the midst of their struggle. Jeremiah had just let the people know that they needed to settle in. Verses 5–6 told them to build houses and live in them; plant gardens and eat of the harvest; get married and have babies. They were not expecting that verse 11 would mean they would instantly go to their promised land. In context, they knew they were settling into a place that wasn't meant for them forever.

The point of Jeremiah 29:11 is that we learn who God is, not what is about to happen to us. We learn that God knows the plans He has for us. I still get slightly irritated when I hear this verse quoted without the full context. God knew the plan, but my life feeling a little stuck in exile, much like the Israelites', seemed a bit cruel. Then I began to understand the context that verses 12–14 offer: "Then you will call upon me and come and pray to me, and I will hear you. You will seek me and find me, when you seek me with all your heart. I will be found by you, declares the LORD, and I will restore your fortunes and gather you from all the nations and all the places where I have driven you, declares the LORD, and I will bring you back to the place from which I sent you into exile."

Again, this tells us about God: He can hear us, He can be found, He can restore, and He can bring back. All we have to do is seek Him. Are you seeking God or just going through life on autopilot? As I read those verses, my understanding of God's intention began to grow. God assures us that He knows the plans for our lives and wants us to seek Him. Not the internet, a friend, a family member, an article, or a specialist—none of those people or things can do what God can do. I'm not saying that we shouldn't pursue wisdom and talent, but we are to pursue God and His will first, above all else.

To clarify, seeking isn't a stagnant state. Somewhere along the way, we started believing that waiting on or trusting God meant that we did absolutely nothing. Seeking God is not twiddling our thumbs, waiting for Him to move. Our action is required. We will not find God unless we are seeking Him. We will not experience God's purpose until we get up and move.

Someone I dearly love said she once prayed Matthew 7:7–8 to God in a time of questioning whether He was real. Jesus said in those verses, "Ask, and it will be given to you; seek, and you will find; knock, and it will be opened to you. For everyone who asks receives, and the one who seeks finds, and to the one who knocks it will be opened." She said she prayed and prayed, and God never showed Himself. Can you relate? You've wanted your life to have meaning or for a certain mountain to move, and nothing has happened. I'll remind you that the context of Jeremiah 29 is that those people still had to wait seventy years. The Lord tells us, "My thoughts are not your thoughts, neither are your ways my ways. . . . For as the heavens are higher than the earth, so are my ways higher than your ways and my thoughts than your thoughts" (Isaiah 55:8–9).

Ask, the Lord tells us, and it will be given. Are you asking Him, really petitioning Him to come through? Are you brave with your questions? Then He says to seek. Don't just ask; look up. We aren't told that we will find what we asked for, but we are assured that we will find something. You can't stay stuck. You have to get up and start seeking what God has, who He is. Finally, knock. That indicates that we will come up against some closed doors. I hear people pray for God to open doors or refer to a no from God as a closed door. How often do we assume that something shouldn't or can't be because the door is closed? When we come up against closed doors, we need to try knocking. Not all doors are left open; some must be opened for us.

I don't understand God's timing or ways. I don't know why you are stuck or how long the feeling of being stagnant will last. But I do know that Jesus followed up in Matthew 7 with this: "Or which of you, if his son asks him for bread, will give him a stone? Or if he asks for a fish, will give him a serpent? If you then, who are evil, know how to give good gifts to your children, how much more will your Father who is in heaven give good things to those who ask him!" (vv. 9–11).

Those verses might sting some of you because you struggle with trusting and believing in God. After all, you couldn't trust or believe your earthly parents. When you hear things like "how much more" about the Father's love for you compared to your earthly parents' love, it does nothing for you but stir up hurt. I'm so sorry for that, so deeply sorry. I hope we can all grow in our belief that our heavenly Father is lavishly good. Don't give up asking and seeking His purpose for you.

So how do we get unstuck and off our hamster wheel and choose to chase after our purpose?

First, seek God. I know that seems like a no-brainer, but how often do we not ask because we don't want to be a burden to God? Or how often do we become so busy going round and round that we never think to pause and see if we are doing His thing or our own? Take a minute and pause to ask God before you do things. This simple act of surrender can turn the most mundane tasks into purpose. I used to work at our church, and one day one of the pastors asked me if I could help him with something. He had a bunch of letters to send out, and he needed help stuffing the envelopes. Then he said something that changed how I did mundane tasks: "As you stuff each envelope and seal it, say a prayer for the family that will receive it." I hadn't thought that something so little could become so significant. I don't do this for everything I do, but I do it often, and it has revolutionized the most mundane moments. Couldn't you do the same as you stuff Christmas cards into envelopes? Or as you fold a load of laundry, what if you prayed over the person (even if it's your-self) who will wear each item? As you sit in traffic, on the bus, or in the subway station, what if you started praying for the strangers you pass on your commute? The same can be true of the people you scroll past on social media, when you send emails, or after (or on) phone calls. This simple practice can invite God into your day. It brings you back to reality while transcending it because you are bringing heaven to earth.

During what mundane tasks or times could you begin implementing this idea?

Second, take a step (or steps) of faith. We can stay stuck too often because we are waiting for certainty. Certainty isn't faith. Again, we often want a very clear sign from God instead of being willing to trust what we can't yet see. Like modern-day Stepford wives, we are going through the motions we think we should do. Sometimes we don't take steps because we are afraid we will take the wrong ones. I totally relate to this fear, and I'll be honest here even if it's not encouraging: you will take some wrong steps. *But God can* lead you back to His better way. If you go down one path in faith and it ends up being the wrong one, you have to trust that God will lead you to where He is calling you. God simply will not smite you just because you end up on the wrong path due to taking a step of faith. This ideology is consistent with all that we learn about God in His Word. (Taking a step in the wrong direction accidentally is not to be confused with disobedience. But even with that, didn't God swallow up Jonah and spit him out where he should have gone? One way or another, God will lead us to His path. Let's start this journey with a step of faith.)

Is there anything you are fearful or anxious about that might keep you from taking a step of faith?

Later on we will discuss when we should wait, when we should take baby steps, and how to take giant leaps of faith. Before we take that deep dive, let's start to scratch the surface of this concept.

Maybe the saying shouldn't be, "You can't, *but God can*." A truer phrase might be, "You could, *but God can* do it better." Yes, you are a wildly competent woman. You've likely accomplished and become so many things because you are so capable. But just because you can doesn't mean you should. I would likely relate to the "I can, so I'll just do it" group best. I've learned—rather, I'm learning—this lesson the hard way. Take it from me; learn from my mistakes. You can, but friend, I promise you that God's way is so much better than you could imagine. Better is not always easier. Better is not always clear. Regardless, it's still better. Don't miss out on God's way because you could make another way yourself.

A while ago, maybe when Karis, my oldest, was a baby, I had become stagnant. I wasn't depressed, but I was for sure stuck. While I loved being a mom with my whole heart, I had gotten a bit lost in this new stage of life. I remember sharing these things with my counselor. She took me to Deuteronomy 30 where Moses was commissioning Joshua to take over leadership of God's people before entering the promised land. "I have set before you life and death, blessing and curse. Therefore choose life, that you and your offspring may live, loving the LORD your God, obeying his voice and holding fast to him, for he is your life and length of days, that you may dwell in the land" (vv. 19–20). She then said, "Becky, you have a choice: you can stay stuck and simply survive this season, or you can choose to thrive in this season. What will it be, life or death?" And so, I ask you the same question, friend. What will it be for you? Death or life? Stagnancy or living out God's purpose for your life? Choose life.

Pray

Father, I confess that I have been stuck in my everyday life, caught up in the whirlwind or the monotony of it all. I need You. I want Your purpose for my life! Help me to seek what You have instead of accepting what is. When I see closed doors, may I not be defeated, but give me the courage to knock. I want to trust You more than I trust myself. I want to choose Your life for me—help me choose life!

Process

1. Do you feel stuck or stagnant in life? How so?
2. Do things or people make you feel too comfortable staying stuck or stagnant? What boundaries could you put up so those are no longer barriers? On the flip side, do things or people encourage you to pursue God's purpose for your life? What could you do to be around them more?
3. What do you think might be the purpose of your life? Be careful not to be stuck on the grandness of this question. We all have many purposes—big and small. What are some of yours right now? (If you aren't sure, this is a great question to get thoughts on from a mentor, family member, or friend.)
4. God calls us to seek Him. Do you have a regular habit of seeking God? There isn't one right way to do this, but we are encouraged all throughout Scripture to seek God frequently. If you don't do that, it is likely the main factor contributing to stagnation. How can you add consistent time with God to your life? Put it on your schedule, set alarms, and get accountability from someone you can depend on to ensure this happens—set yourself up for an abundant life!

Hearers & Doers Challenge

Do one thing to take a step toward your purpose. Don't delay by waiting to find the perfect one. Take a leap of faith! Take one step toward what God might have for you, trusting that if it's not His intended path, He will lead you to a better one.

(8)

YOU FEEL LONELY, BUT GOD IS WITH YOU

Lonely (adjective) / 'lōn-lē
1: being without company: lone; cut off from others: solitary
2: sad from being alone: lonesome
synonyms: alone, deserted, friendless, withdrawn, disassociated,
   quarantined, single[1]

Relationships are rarely easy, and a lack of relationships brings just as many challenges. Many of us are surrounded by people, yet we've never felt so alone (which is the hardest type of loneliness, in my opinion). Sometimes we are lonely because we are so busy we don't have a chance to connect. Sometimes we are lonely because we don't trust others or choose not to be vulnerable with others, and this may be for a good reason—we've been burned. Sometimes we are lonely because there is no one around. Loneliness is something that seems out of our control. In this chapter, I hope to help you see who is in control of everything.

Social media makes us feel even more isolated, which is ironic since it is called "social." Instead of connecting with others, we see all the places we aren't connecting. We see all the things we aren't invited to and see, or at least we think we see, all the fun everyone else is having. Everyone else has their person—everyone but maybe you? Sure, you have friends, but do you really feel known? Safe? Seen? Our real and online lives reaffirm that we are all alone. *But God.*

How about you? Do you feel lonely? Why or why not?

I'm not a relationship expert, so we aren't going to focus on how we can build community. There are plenty of resources for this, both Christian and secular, but psychologically based. Look into those or take the steps you need to take in this area. Here, however, we will focus on loneliness in your relationship with God, which is intensified when you already feel lonely in daily life.

Just as we can feel lonely when others surround us, we can also feel lonely even though we know God is everywhere. Since He isn't tangible, we can often miss Him. But the opposite is also true: when we feel really known by our Father, even when we have relationally lonely seasons, we can feel seen, known, and loved because of our intimacy with Him. This isn't to say we don't need others; the Bible is very clear on the value of community.

Earlier we looked at Adam and Eve. Recall that after they had eaten the fruit and hid, God asked them, "Where are you?" In this chapter, we will flip the question and ask God where He has been and now is. We often wonder where God is or why He allowed a certain thing to happen when we are in or have experienced a hard season. I know this is something I struggled with before becoming a Christian. And if I'm honest, I have struggled with it since.

I'd gone to church my whole life, but I didn't become a Christian until I was sixteen and heard the story of Lazarus dying. I want us to go back to this story because it shows that God hasn't abandoned us, even if it seems that way. It's also a fantastic reminder of the importance of inviting others in.

Lazarus and his sisters, Mary and Martha, were good friends of Jesus. We are told in John 11 that Jesus loved them. The verse that first catches us a little off guard in this chapter is verse 6: "So, when he [Jesus] heard that Lazarus was ill, he stayed two days longer in the place where he was." To be clear, Jesus was in a different town than his friends Mary, Martha, and Lazarus. Mary and Martha had sent word to Jesus because Lazarus was sick, and Jesus intentionally didn't go to help. Can you relate to how Mary and Martha might have felt? Has there been a time when you wanted Jesus to show up and He didn't? Maybe you're experiencing such a time right now.

By the time Jesus arrived, he had discovered that Lazarus had died and had already been in the tomb for four days. When Martha heard that Jesus was almost there, she went and met him on the way. In verses 21–22, she responded honestly: "Lord, if you had been here, my brother would not have died. But even now I know that whatever you ask from God, God will give you." Martha was so honest and still so filled with faith. Can't you hear her? Haven't you been her? If Jesus had only shown up for you, then none of that would have happened. That's how Martha felt. If only Jesus had come sooner, then Lazarus wouldn't have died. But he was too late. Martha then let her sister know that Jesus had come, and Mary quickly got up to see Jesus. Like her sister, her first response to Jesus was, "Lord, if you had been here, my brother would not have died" (v. 32). Where was Jesus? Why hadn't He come? Jesus had left them all alone, and Lazarus died.

Next in this story is the verse everyone loves to memorize and the verse that changed my entire life: "Jesus wept" (v. 35). I've since studied this very short verse many times. The first time I heard it, I also wept. Instead of being mad at God for feeling like He had abandoned me, I realized He'd been there all along and that my pain brought Him pain. He actually cared. The Greek word here for *wept* is that guttural cry—the kind that is loud, deep, and expressive. This was not a quiet, single tear trickling down His cheek.

What happened next was nothing short of amazing. Jesus went with everyone to the tomb where Lazarus had been buried. He then instructed them to move the stone. Martha, sweet Martha, was very quick to say that maybe they shouldn't do that because it would smell bad. You are right, Martha, relationships can be messy and stinky sometimes. Even so, Jesus had the stone removed. And then He commanded, "Lazarus, come out" (v. 43). And we see in verse 44 that "the man who had died came out, his hands and feet bound with linen strips, and his face wrapped with a cloth. Jesus said to them, 'Unbind him, and let him go.'"

Whoa. Jesus had seemingly abandoned them. They all, including Jesus, grieved the passing of Lazarus. *But God.* Jesus did what only He can do: He raised what was once dead.

The last thing we see Jesus do is pull the community back in. He knows we desperately need others. Jesus brought Lazarus new life, but Lazarus was still bound in his burial clothes. Jesus didn't take those off; instead, He told the people there to do it. That's our job—we are meant to unbind one another and encourage one another to live life abundantly.

One of the most profound parts of this story is the question that both Mary and Martha asked Jesus: "Where were you? If you'd only been here!" I went to a counselor once who took me through asking Jesus this same question. At first that felt really wrong to do. I didn't think we were supposed to question God. But one of the ways she helped me work through healing was to work through all the times I felt Jesus had abandoned me. And then she had me ask where He had been at that time. Obviously, this isn't a tangible or even a right-or-wrong-answer-approach. This is simply going to the Father and asking for the Spirit to give you an impression of how Jesus was present in a certain moment.

In high school, I experienced something super traumatic. At the end of it, I was left in a stairwell, sobbing, the same way Jesus did when Lazarus died. This has always been a memory that has been triggering for me and has made me question God—His goodness, His presence, and His ability to save us. My counselor took me back to that stairwell and asked, "Becky, where was He? Where was Jesus at that moment?" It took some time, but in my mind, I imagined that Jesus came beside me, sat on the stairs next to me, wrapped His arms around me, and wept with me.

Think through a time when you've wondered where Jesus was. Then take a minute and ask the Spirit to show you where He was. Pause until you can see the physical person of Jesus in the circumstance.

Where was Jesus?

I hope you feel loved. I hope you feel healing coming to a place that once was filled with hurt. I have used this exercise many times to bring healing to memories. I'd encourage you to use it whenever you feel abandoned or hurt by God. I also ask where Jesus is in everyday life circumstances. I look for where He might be at a certain moment. This has been a really sweet way to personify the Trinity.

Again, the last thing we see in this story is that Jesus commissioned people to unbind Lazarus. Having people in our lives is essential to our freedom. Building and maintaining relationships can be stinky, messy, and uncomfortable work. But any relationship that's worth having takes work—we will get our hands dirty.

Who are some valued friends in your life? Are there other people you'd like to try to build a deeper friendship with?

List the friends' names or initials below. Share what makes them good friends, or share how you could be a better friend to them—whatever the Spirit impresses on you.

I don't know if you feel lonely. If you do struggle with loneliness, I hope this new perspective has helped you feel God's nearness more. And I also hope it has inspired you to grow deeper friendships, even if they get messy! Sometimes we experience the presence of God through people. As He brings people into our lives, let's recognize that He might be using them to show His love for us.

Recently I stayed at a cute boutique hotel in Round Top, Texas, to do some uninterrupted writing. I reveled in one of those rare Texas evenings that are perfectly cool without a hint of humidity. Just cool enough to want to be bundled up with a cup of coffee keeping me warm. I was on the back porch with my laptop open and my Bible opened on the rustic farm table when two women came around the corner. They saw my Bible and immediately started talking about their faith. They asked why I was at this hotel, and I told them about writing this book. One of the ladies, Jessica, exuberantly proclaimed, "Oh, let me grab my Bible! We are praying for you! Is that okay?" I had known these women for all of two minutes, and they were pulling up chairs and asking about this book and how they could pray. I told them I wanted to write words that mattered. None of us have time to waste, but we all desperately need to hear from the Father, and we all need to walk freely in the way He has called us to. Then these women grabbed my hands with Bibles in their laps, and they prayed the most beautiful prayer over us (I say us, because they prayed for you too). I never saw those women again; they were off the next morning before I woke up. I didn't have more conversations with them, nor did they become my people. My loneliness hadn't changed, but I had never felt so seen by the Lord.

> Can you think of a time when you've experienced something similar? Maybe you felt alone, but God did something to fill that void.

God promises in Isaiah 41:10, "Fear not, for I am with you; be not dismayed, for I am your God; I will strengthen you, I will help you, I will uphold you with my righteous right hand." While you might feel lonely, you are never alone—God is with you.

Pray

Father, I ask that You bring healing to the times when I felt You had abandoned me. Show me where You were in those moments. Bring healing to places that are hurt. I also ask that You bring people to be the kind of friends that unbind, even if it's messy. Help me to be that for others too. Thank You for your presence! Help me to sense You even when I can't see You.

Process

1. How does it feel to know that you were prayed for by me but also by total strangers more than a year before you'd ever hold this book? You couldn't have even known you'd have this book one day. *But God.* You were already on His mind!

2. Do you feel lonely? What makes you feel lonely? How have you found feelings of loneliness?

3. What was the most significant or surprising thing you discovered from doing the exercise of seeing where Jesus was in a time when you once felt hurt or abandoned?

4. What is your biggest takeaway from the story of Lazarus?

Hearers & Doers Challenge

We worked a bit on our relationship with Jesus. So for your challenge here, set up an intentional time with a friend. Maybe you simply set up a coffee date, but you go in with some questions that would help them be unbound. Or maybe you reach out to some friends and see if they'd like to meet for accountability every week. Take a step toward building a strong community base.

9

YOU FEEL DISQUALIFIED, BUT GOD MAKES YOU NEW

Disqualify (verb) / dis-ˈkwä-lə-ˌfī

1: to deprive of the required qualities, properties, or conditions: make unfit

2: to deprive of a power, right, or privilege

synonyms: ineligible, incapable, unfit, unskilled, inept, useless, worthless[1]

Recently I snapped a picture of my view and sent it to my hubs and bestie. Just over a year ago, I sat at this same table with a friend to talk about becoming a Realtor. I've always been a multipassionate person. I have a passion for coaching women one-on-one and for being an all-in wife and mom, but I also love things that involve business strategy, especially consulting. I've also always wanted to be a Realtor. It's a side interest that, at the time, I thought might need to become my main interest. I was meeting with my friend to learn more about being a Realtor because I didn't think I had what it took to do the ministry work I had felt called to. Failure, rejection, insecurity, and what felt like a thousand other things made me feel disqualified from this work. Along with the picture of the same table, I told them, "A year ago, I sat at this very table. I was ready to quit ministry and felt so very disqualified. On my own, I was done. On my own, I couldn't. On my own, I couldn't see another way. *But God can!*" If I had quit, I would have missed out on all the Lord had planned. You might not even realize where you've disqualified yourself, or maybe you know exactly.

Take a moment and identify where you've felt disqualified:
These can be things from your past and present.

Hope is coming, friend—God is making a new way! I'm living in the newness that only He can offer, and I'm getting giddy thinking about what your story will be like a year from now. What might you share if you choose to believe and receive the new things God has for you and stop believing the lie that you've been disqualified?

I'm not a crier. I wish I were. However, the first time I heard Kelly Clarkson sing the acoustic version of her song "Piece by Piece" on *American Idol*, I wept. In fact, I can still pull it up on YouTube and sob. In this song, she says about her dad, "But your love, it isn't free; it has to be earned. Back then, I didn't have anything you needed, so I was worthless."[2] When she said that last word, "worthless," she broke, and so did I.

Worthless. Didn't that perfectly describe how I felt? Isn't it the way so many of us feel?

Kelly was singing about her dad, but a hundred other things, both from our past and in our present, tell us we are worthless. Maybe when we were growing up, a parent's words or lack of presence told us we were worthless. We look at our bank account and feel worthless. Or even with our arms full of possessions we feel worthless. We look in the mirror, taking in every flaw, and see ourselves as worthless. We look at our dating history or struggling marriage and see ourselves as worthless. We look at our career, where it hasn't gone, and even where it has gone, and think we are worthless. We look at our children's behavior, and we are worthless. We could go on for pages and pages, recounting all the ways we've deemed ourselves worthless. That might seem dramatic, but I want us to be honest about what we speak and think about ourselves. Too often we allow the state of a part of our life to determine our whole worth. We have 20/20 vision for everything that disqualifies us from being loved and created for a purpose by God, and we desperately need new lenses to see ourselves as God sees us.

One of my favorite Bible stories that illustrates this is the story of Moses being called by God in Exodus 3. Moses would eventually do astonishing things and intimately know God. But we must remember that Moses did not know then what we know now. He was just like us, a very ordinary person loved by an extraordinary God.

When Moses was a baby, all newborn Israelite boys were being killed, but his mother saved his life by helping him become the child of Pharaoh's daughter. While this protected Moses' life, it also drastically changed it. We can confidently assume that Moses never truly belonged. He no longer fit in with the Israelites, nor was he an Egyptian—disqualified from ever really belonging. After growing up, he witnessed all the hardships the Egyptians inflicted on his people, the Israelites. In a moment of rage, he killed an Egyptian after witnessing him beating an Israelite. He was found out, and out of fear, he ran away—disqualifying himself from his place in the palace. Years passed, and Moses married and was living as a shepherd.

One day while Moses was out with his flock, the angel of the Lord appeared to him from a flame of fire in a bush. I know that's a little hard to believe, *but God can* show up any way He wants. Well, for Moses, it got even harder to believe. The Lord told Moses that He had seen the suffering of Moses' people and wanted to send Moses to Egypt to free them from Pharaoh. You'd think that given the angel and the fire that didn't consume the bush, Moses would immediately have said yes. But he didn't.

"Who am I that I should go to Pharaoh?" Moses asked (Exodus 3:11). Moses knew exactly who he was, and he had already disqualified himself from this job.

The Lord responded, "But I will be with you" (3:12). God didn't need Moses to have a certain level of faith or a certain résumé. All He needed was for him to say yes and then go. But even when God is speaking directly to someone through a fire, it's hard to hear His voice above the voice of the lying Enemy.

So Moses asked another question: Who would he tell the Egyptians had sent him? To which God then powerfully proclaimed Himself as "I AM WHO I AM," and told Moses to go (3:13–14).

Instead of immediately complying, Moses made some excuses. "They [Moses' fellow Israelites] will not believe me or listen to my voice, for they will say, 'The LORD did not appear to you'" (4:1). The Lord then gave Moses two signs. He turned his staff into a snake and made his hand leprous.

Moses still did not listen to the Lord. He had another excuse: "Oh, my Lord, I am not eloquent, either in the past or since you have spoken to your servant, but I am slow of speech and of tongue" (4:10). The Lord then reminded Moses that He had created Moses' mouth and would teach him what to speak. And again He told Moses to go.

Moses just couldn't accept that the Lord chose him to free the Israelites. So he put up another petition in verse 13, this time sounding more desperate than ever: "Oh, my Lord, please send someone else." And this was when the Lord began to become angry. Nevertheless, He conceded and told Moses that Aaron, his brother, could accompany him. Finally, Moses went.

With our hindsight, Moses' objections seem ridiculous. For we know that Moses, with Aaron's help, would go up against Pharaoh ten times, resulting in ten plagues. And then he would lead the people across the sea on dry ground toward their promised land. He also would meet with God on the mountain to receive His commandments, resulting in his face shining from being in God's very presence. We know what was possible for Moses, but Moses could see only what was.

> **Write "but God can" statements to your list of disqualifications.**
>
> Example: "I came from a divorced home, and our premarital counselor said we'd never make it, *but God can* give (and has given) me an amazing hubby. Yes, our marriage is far from perfect, but he's still my favorite person to be around. Yes, we have to work on our relationship all the time (the marriage counselor wasn't wrong that it would be hard), but God sustained us to celebrate fifteen years of marriage recently!"

I closely resonate with Moses on his specific petitions. I am constantly disqualifying myself. I'll be honest—what I expose myself to does a number on me. Years ago, magazines brought me down, and now it's social media. I see all that other people are doing that's similar to what I'm doing, and I think that I won't ever catch up to or be as great as them. I forget that I'm seeing their highlight reel or a highly edited image. I turn from those pages or the screen to disqualify myself: *I'll never be as good a mom as she is. I'll never be the wife that she is. I'll never have that six-pack like she has after having all the kids.* Disqualified, disqualified, disqualified.

I love learning from Paul in the Bible because he readily admitted what a mess he had been. He had killed Christians! While he was a Jew among Jews, he was absolutely detestable to Christians. *But God.* Jesus appeared to him one day, and everything changed. The same has happened in my life, and I'm sure yours also if you are part of God's family. I once was disqualified, but God made me new.

As a communicator, I connected with Moses' words about not being able to have the right words. His problem was that he was focused on himself. Now, almost every time before I teach, I pray the words of Paul over myself. He wrote in 1 Corinthians 2:1–5, "And I, when I came to you, brothers, did not come proclaiming to you the testimony of God with lofty speech or wisdom. For I decided to know nothing among you except Jesus Christ and him crucified. And I was with you in weakness and in fear and much trembling, and my speech and my message were not in plausible words of wisdom, but in demonstration of the Spirit and of power, so that your faith might not rest in the wisdom of men but in the power of God." It's okay if I write with a ton of fragments or run-on sentences strung together. It's okay if I say "um" when I speak or if I speak with too much passion. It's not about me; it's about God! And when I put my faith in Him each time I step on a stage or open a blank document to start writing, I trust He will use my weakness to show His power.

The truth is there are better communicators than me, much better. But God, for whatever reason, likes to use my jumbled mess so that people don't put their faith in me but in Him. With that in mind, I want to share some verses about what God says about you. All the disqualifications you shared above are like Moses saying he didn't speak well or asking if people would believe him. You feel disqualified, *but God* makes you new.

- "Remember not the former things, nor consider the things of old" (Isaiah 43:18).
- "We all, with unveiled face, beholding the glory of the Lord, are being transformed into the same image from one degree of glory to another. For this comes from the Lord who is the Spirit" (2 Corinthians 3:18).
- "If anyone is in Christ, he is a new creation. The old has passed away; behold, the new has come" (2 Corinthians 5:17).
- "I have been crucified with Christ. It is no longer I who live, but Christ who lives in me. And the life I now live in the flesh I live by faith in the Son of God, who loved me and gave himself for me" (Galatians 2:20).
- "You have . . . put on the new self, which is being renewed in knowledge after the image of its creator" (Colossians 3:9–10).

I know you see all the reasons you use to disqualify yourself. But I hope you get that Jesus knows all of that, and He still died for you and rose again so that you could have a new life.

I met with a mentor, Sandy, a year ago, and I was going through a season where I couldn't stop playing all my disqualifications on repeat. At one point, I told her, "I just want to be used by God."

"Ah, there's the problem," she said. What? What was the problem? I wanted to be used by God. I wanted my life to mean something to God. What was wrong with that? While the Bible does absolutely support good works, it doesn't support them at the sacrifice of faith. She said to me, "Becky, have you ever considered that God doesn't want to use you? He wants to be known by you."

I was speechless. No. No, I had not ever once considered that. I didn't understand how He could love me just for knowing Him and not for serving Him. The greatest commandment blew my theory out of the water, right? When Jesus was pressed about which was the greatest commandment, He replied, "You shall love the Lord your God with all your heart and with all your soul and with all your mind" (Matthew 22:37). He did not say, "Do *this*" or "Be *that*." No, He said the most important thing you can do is love Him with all of yourself. What if, instead of trying to live in a way to qualify ourselves, we live as Jesus has actually made us new and show Him how much we love Him?

The song "Piece by Piece" ends with these words, and just before Kelly Clarkson sang them, she broke again, and so did I: "He'll never walk away, he'll never break her heart. He'll take care of things; he'll love her. Piece by piece, he restored my faith that a man can be kind and a father should be great."[3] For me, this song has never been about a man; instead, the song's hero has always been Jesus. That's what He did for me. I had my life crushed by others and had also personally crushed my life into a broken mess. Then piece by piece, Jesus put me together into something brand-new. And this new creation that I had become wasn't meant to be used by Him but to love Him and be loved by Him.

Pray

Father, I confess that I have believed disqualifying lies about myself. [Go back to the list of things you thought disqualified you and write "All Things New" on top of them.] Thank You for making me new! Give me the courage to see myself as You see me. I don't want to live believing things that are no longer true about myself. Help me to see myself the way You see me.

Process

1. Is there a song that resonates with you in describing your story or life? How so?

2. How do you feel when you believe disqualifications about yourself? How has believing the disqualifications limited you?

3. Of all the verses about being new, which one do you connect with the most? Are there other verses that describe your transformation with the Lord? What are they?

4. Do you struggle, like I have, to believe that loving God is enough?

Hearers & Doers Challenge

Take note for the next week whenever you disqualify yourself. Then do the steps we did before: write a new truth and add your "But God can" to your disqualification. Stop and thank God each time for what He has done and is doing.

(10)

YOU FEEL OVERWHELMED, BUT GOD SENDS A HELPER

overwhelmed (verb) / ō-vər-ˈ(h)welmd

1: overcome by force or numbers

2: completely overcome or overpowered by thought or feeling

synonyms: swamped, overcame, drowned, overmastered,

   crushed[1]

When someone asks how we are, we often give one of two common responses: "I'm good" or "Oh, I've just been so busy." Busyness is our personal badge of honor that we simultaneously hate wearing. Older women, however, sometimes struggle with a lack of busyness. For so long, it is what overwhelms us, and then once life calms down, that, too, overwhelms us.

I remember being a young mom in the grocery store. Four-year-old Karis would be talking up a storm, crossing things off my list, and begging to get out of the cart. Moriah, a full-on two year old, was next to her, either making best friends with everyone we passed or hitting Karis and telling her to stop treating her like a baby because she was a big girl. And then I had Chandler strapped to my body, either sound asleep because third kids know how to sleep anywhere, or screaming at the top of her lungs because she was done with being along for the ride. Every time we went to the store, I was guaranteed to be stopped by at least one woman coming down the aisle, who, when she would see my crew, would give us a gentle smile with a distant look of fondness washing over her. When she'd reach us, she'd stop as if what she was about to tell me would burst out of her if she didn't. Sometimes she'd pat strapped-to-my-body Chandler on the back as she said, "Oh, savor these days! They go too quickly." I'd smile back and say, "Yes, ma'am," and then continue down the aisle. Some days I'd do my best not to think maybe she was delusional and she'd forgotten how hard this was. And other days I'd continue down the aisle, take a deep breath, and remind myself that the days are long, but the years are so very short.

Now my girls are a bit older. If they get in the cart now, it's because they climbed over the sides into the larger section; their being there is more comical than necessary. Actually, we hardly go into the grocery store anymore. Life is still busy, just in a different way. Now I order online and swing by the store to pick up groceries between all the practices, appointments, and carpool lines.

You don't realize how fast the years go when you are stuck in very long days. Not until those years have passed in a blink of an eye. I get those sweet older women now. Every time a younger friend of mine texts me a photo of her baby wearing or playing with something we handed down to them, I ache a little. Those days seemed so hard, so never-ending. I was overwhelmed. And now I would do anything for those seemingly slower days again, just as my mamaw and mother-in-law have told me how they ache for the days of driving kids everywhere and the wildness of the teen years. They miss the noise and the shut-tling around. The silence is the thing that overwhelms them now.

We all have different things that overwhelm us—busyness and stillness, singleness and marriage, no money and so much money, fit-ness and sickness. What I hope you realize with greater confidence after reading this chapter is that you are not alone in any of it: you have a Helper.

I don't know how many women's events I have attended where we learned about Mary and Martha from Luke 10:38–42. Generally the story was summarized like this: Martha was grumpy, pouty, and very busy, while Mary did the best and simply sat listening at Jesus' feet. While that isn't entirely wrong, I hope I can give you a slightly different lens to view this story through.

The first thing we see in this story is that "Martha welcomed him [Jesus] into her house" (v. 38). I want to ensure that we give Martha some credit for this, even though she soon got caught up in serving. She was leading her household well; she was the one who made space for Jesus. This is where I want us to learn to think differently about ourselves and stop the lying voice of shame, even if it holds a hint of truth. Martha welcomed Jesus in. Friend, even if you've done nothing else recently, picking up this book is one way you've welcomed Jesus into your life as well.

Next in the story, we see Mary, "who sat at the Lord's feet and listened to his teaching" (v. 39). I didn't have a sister growing up, but I have three girls now and can totally see how this next part plays out. The camera turns to Martha, who we are told was "distracted with much serving" (v. 40). She approaches Jesus and says, "Lord, do you not care that my sister has left me to serve alone? Tell her then to help me" (v. 40). Sometimes I think it would be helpful if the Bible showed dialogue like drama script. I imagine the response from Martha was more like this:

SCENE: Martha is intermittently in the kitchen stirring various pots while leaving to fold laundry, tidy bedrooms, and ensure other tasks are covered since she has guests. Meanwhile Mary sits on the floor in the living room, listening to Jesus talk.

MARTHA: (giant sigh with one hand on her hip and the other waving around erratically) "Looord!" (voice escalating with each letter and waving her arms at Mary) "Do yooou not care that" (turning toward Mary, gritting her teeth, and speaking through pursed lips) "my siiiiister has left me" (voice at highest volume, both hands in the air) "to serve alone?!" (lowering her voice while stomping her feet and pointing at Mary) "Tell herrr" (full-on pout mode, and gesturing to herself now) "to help me!" (*sniff, sniff* with a justified look on her face)

I could be wrong about this, but I do have three girls, and I've heard this very argument before.

Martha gets a bad rap in this story for her outburst and busyness, but in truth, she was doing what was common for women and was most certainly expected of her in that day. She hadn't gotten in trouble because she was serving; she got into a bad place because she was "*distracted* with *much* serving" (v. 40, emphasis mine). Ouch. Does that sting a little for you too? Serving and doing aren't bad things. Look at the highly praised Proverbs 31 woman—she had *a lot* going on. What Jesus was after here with Martha wasn't to get her to sit just like Mary but to choose her good portion just like Mary.

Choose is the Greek word *eklegomai*, and it means just what you think it means: to make a choice.[2] Jesus was pointing out to Mary that she had a choice: she could be distracted by whatever she was doing or she could learn from Jesus.

How are you like Martha in this story? How are you like Mary?

Put together a plan for how you will to spend time in God's Word, in prayer, and connecting with Him throughout your day. Having a plan or intention gives us a framework to grow within. Then we remember to be flexible and give ourselves grace because life most certainly happens.

Jesus used this same word for *choose* in John's gospel: "No longer do I call you servants, for the servant does not know what his master is doing; but I have called you friends, for all that I have heard from my Father I have made known to you. You did not choose me, but I chose you and appointed you that you should go and bear fruit and that your fruit should abide, so that whatever you ask the Father in my name, he may give it to you. These things I command you, so that you will love one another" (15:15–17). So often, as we interpret this passage about Martha, we frame busyness as bad. Martha wasn't rebuked for her busyness but for her distraction. The truth is, if Mary had been sitting in her room scrolling on social media instead of sitting at Jesus' feet, she, too, would have been rebuked for being distracted by her stillness.

We learn in John 15 that Jesus doesn't want us to live like servants but as friends. He doesn't want us to be overwhelmed by all we have to do for Him or for others. Instead, He wants us to take the posture of a friend—to sit with Him so that we can "go and bear fruit" (v. 16). He is not asking you to stop everything. That's not the lesson to learn here. But, friend, He doesn't want you overwhelmed by your life either.

In John 16:7 and 13, Jesus continued on by saying that we aren't alone in our sitting or our going, our stillness or our busyness—He is sending the Helper. That name would sound familiar to them because He had just taught them, in John 14:16 and verses 26–27, "I will ask the Father, and he will give you another Helper, to be with you forever. . . . But the Helper, the Holy Spirit, whom the Father will send in my name, he will teach you all things and bring to your remembrance all that I have said to you. Peace I leave with you; my peace I give to you. Not as the world gives do I give to you. Let not your hearts be troubled, neither let them be afraid." You aren't alone; Jesus has given you a Helper.

Many of us don't really know what to do with the Helper. I've heard people say before that the Trinity they learned was Father, Son, and Holy Scriptures (instead of Spirit). They are kidding . . . sort of. We like the Scriptures because they are tangible, while the Spirit is ethereal. How do we get help from someone we can't see, touch, or hear? That's where the Scriptures come in; they allow us to learn about the Spirit and see how the Helper has helped people. There isn't a right or wrong way to connect with the Helper.

I remember reading *The Shack* by William Paul Young many years ago (this isn't an endorsement of the book). It is a work of fiction; you won't find it used in theology classes at seminaries. Even so, it greatly shaped how I tangibly view the Trinity. Without giving away too many details, a man finds himself in a cabin in the woods. What makes this cabin unusual is that the people who live in the cabin are God the Father (a larger Black woman who talks with a Southern drawl and acts just like you'd want a mom to act), God the Son (a super laid-back, philosophical young Arab man likely appearing much like Jesus looked but in carpenter pants and Birkenstocks), and God the Spirit (a super serene Asian woman who appears everywhere, knows just what to say, and helps create the most beautiful things). Throughout the course of the book, and now the movie, you see the man begin to adjust to these human versions of the Trinity. Reading the book first, then seeing it played out in the movie helped me understand what my relationship with the Trinity could be. The Trinity isn't so far out of reach; the fictional characters wanted the same kind of interaction I experience with my husband, kids, and closest friends. They wanted to live people's everyday lives with them.

How can you be more like Mary and choose the better thing, time at Jesus' feet?

I don't have enough space here to explain how to connect with the Spirit, but you don't need a guide anyway. Just start. The Spirit is a Helper, and He helps us go and bear fruit. Since we are all called to go to different places and bear different fruit, we can't expect how we interact with the Helper to be the same. For me, it's inviting the Helper into my day. It's talking to the Helper as a person with me to help along the way.

Whether you are walking your figurative aisles alone or you have a lot of life surrounding you or strapped to you, you don't have to live overwhelmed. You aren't alone—you, my friend, have a Helper.

Pray

Father, Jesus, and my Helper, thank You for not leaving me alone. Help me to know You—all of You, all parts of the Trinity, not just the parts I'm comfortable with. Teach me to come to You when I feel overwhelmed. Show me how to walk with You so I don't even get to the place where I am overwhelmed. Thank You for not leaving me on my own to figure things out. Help me lean on You and follow Your way in my busyness and rest.

Process

1. Do you feel overwhelmed by your life right now? How so? (Note: Just as I mentioned, how we feel overwhelmed changes.

I felt overwhelmed when I had young kids, but now that sounds dreamy. Now I feel overwhelmed having three preteens, but I'm sure I will long for these days when they are teens and in college. I felt overwhelmed trying to get a book deal, and I can also feel overwhelmed by all the words I still had to write before the deadline. Does that make sense? Don't compare your life to the past or to others' lives. How do you feel today?)

2. How might the perspective I provided of the story of Mary and Martha change how you see busyness?

3. What do you feel you are choosing right now? Are you distracted or choosing what's best? And how can you choose the better portion? What would that look like?

4. How do you connect best with the Helper?

Hearers & Doers Challenge

As we discussed, there isn't a right or really even a wrong way to connect with the Helper. I've found it's a bit of trial and error, and it changes some in different seasons of life. I have also found it helpful to get friends and mentors to advise me. Your challenge for this chapter is to text, email, and/or post on social media asking others to share how they connect with and get help from the Holy Spirit.

YOU FEEL INADEQUATE, BUT GOD SAYS YOU ARE WORTHY

Inadequate (adjective) / i-ˈna-di-kwət

1: not adequate: not enough or good enough: insufficient

2: not capable

synonyms: deficient, lacking, scarce, insufficient, short, unsatisfactory[1]

I am about to share a story with you that I have shared with only a few trusted friends. I am already nervous because this story will show how ridiculous I am. So even though I'm pulling you into my inner circle by sharing this story with you, know you have full permission to laugh at my ridiculousness. Okay, I'm stalling. Can you tell I'm stalling?

Every couple of years, I go on a retreat, Feminine Hearts Alive, with the purpose of restoring my connection with the Father. During the retreat, participants identify lies we've believed about ourselves. At the end of the trip, we ask God to give us a new name. On the second day of the trip, we identify the main lie we've believed about ourselves. I already shared with you that my core lie is "not enough." Well, one year I experienced a rejection I didn't anticipate and showed up to the retreat feeling defeated. So when we were asked to write the lie we believed then, the word came easily: *inadequate.* I felt completely and utterly not good enough, incapable, and insufficient. The Father knew I needed to be there after getting that crushing news.

Strategy is my superpower. If you need someone to brainstorm ideas, I'm your girl. I also have a background in public relations if you need to twist something. Thankfully, the Lord has quite a sense of humor and abundant patience with my ridiculousness. Since I'd already been to this retreat a few times, I knew I'd need to trade in *inadequate* for something different, a truth-filled new name. I had about fifteen minutes before that specific session started, and since it was nice out, I decided to go for a little walk. Many would use that time to take in the beautiful scenery—fog-filled fields, horses, an old dirt road, and rolling hills just past the lake. This is what meditation dreams are made of. So naturally, instead of being chill, I turned it into a brainstorm with the Lord about my new name.

I asked Him to show me, and the name came instantly. One problem: I couldn't receive it. The name I sensed in my spirit was the name of my favorite Bible teacher and writer of the best Bible studies and books. To accept this name felt absolutely ridiculous. I immediately offered God other options.

I thought closer antonyms might be better options for my new name: sufficient, enough, anything but the name I had just sensed. I was in total denial. I could've accepted those synonyms, but this name made me feel like an imposter. I knew we would write our new names on a board at the front of the room for all to see. How in the world could I write this very well-known name down for all to see? How pious, how weird, how audacious. I couldn't. The truth is, I wasn't inadequate and I could have taken the name "More Than Enough." Don't you know I tried. However, the Lord, in His lavish goodness, wanted me to know how worthy I am. I didn't know what to do with this, so I went into full-on negotiating mode. Yes, I attempted to negotiate with God, as if my ideas would be helpful to Him. (Please, friend, tell me you are laughing at me.)

Finally, He granted me a compromise. While this woman's name is well-known by many, she has a nickname few knew. As a final attempt, I offered this nickname to the Lord as an option: Wanda. I was shaking with laughter as I returned to my pew in the chapel—at myself, the Lord, the name, all of it. It was a bit like when Sarah laughed at the Lord in Genesis 18:12. Her laughter was an acknowledgment that God could do the impossible and the ridiculous. We may see ourselves as inadequate, and that label may feel reasonable given our circumstances. Yet, notice that the Lord doesn't want you to see yourself simply as enough. He will go to great measures to help change your self-perception from inadequate to worthy. Just as you might feel uncomfortable in the presence of a celebrity, royalty, something highly valuable, or a renowned anything, you might also feel uncomfortable with the name He gives you. If He gave you the name Wanda, it might have felt like an insult, but for me it will be something I treasure forever.

What about you—in what ways do you feel not enough?

List any areas or ways you feel inadequate.

The story of the woman caught in adultery (John 8:1–11) breaks and warms my heart. Jesus was teaching on the temple steps, and the scribes and Pharisees brought a woman to Him who had been caught in adultery. Some scholars say she might not even have been clothed to bring further disgrace—her sins made bare for all to see. Those religious leaders told Jesus that the law said she could be stoned for her sin, and then they asked Him what they should do. They did this to test Jesus. Then Jesus bent down and wrote something in the dirt on the ground. (Oh, how I wish we could know what it is that He wrote.) Then he said to those leaders who were ready to kill this woman for what she had done, "Let him who is without sin among you be the first to throw a stone at her" (v. 7). These leaders prided themselves on keeping the law perfectly. But even they walked away one by one. Then this woman, in all her shame and inadequacy, was left with Jesus. He rose and said to her, "Woman, where are they? Has no one condemned you?" (v. 10). She responded, "No one, Lord." And then Jesus, in all of His goodness and grace, replied, "Neither do I condemn you; go, and from now on sin no more" (v. 11).

The law was on the side of the scribes and Pharisees. This woman knew that death was a likely outcome that day. Not all of us are in relationships like this or have had people who speak condemnation over us, but some of us have. Those words can sting, and the scar can last a lifetime. As children we are told, "Sticks and stones may break my bones, but words will never hurt me." But there isn't any truth in that, is there? The negative words someone has told us can somehow stick with us more than a hundred positive words.

Have any words been spoken over you that have hurt you? List what you can remember.

Think back to childhood and relationships that have hurt, and record anything you can remember that has hurt you.

I'm so sorry anyone ever said those things to you. I've found in my life that it's not the stones others are ready to throw at me or have thrown at me that sting the most, but the ones I throw at myself. Too often I walk around bruised or weighed down by the stones I've thrown at myself or carried around. Friend, it's time to lay down those stones that we aim at ourselves.

What stones have you thrown at yourself?
List anything you say about yourself to shame or punish yourself. This can be anything—whatever you say that you would never allow a friend to say about themself.

God's truth also says that you don't stand condemned. "There is therefore now no condemnation for those who are in Christ Jesus. For the law of the Spirit of life has set you free in Christ Jesus from the law of sin and death. For God has done what the law, weakened by the flesh, could not do" (Romans 8:1–3). Under the law, that woman could have been killed. *But God.* Jesus stepped in and defended her, just as He does you. Every condemnatory thing that comes against you—whether valid or not—is null and void because of Jesus. He has called you to live and be free! Doesn't that sound good? When He looks at you, He doesn't see what you might see; He calls you worthy. Here are a few verses that remind us of how special we are to the Father.

- Psalm 139:14 says that we are fearfully and wonderfully made.

- Zephaniah 3:17 says that the Lord takes great delight in us, so much that He rejoices over us with singing.
- Luke 12:6–7 tells us that God values even the sparrows, and we are much more valuable than they. He loves us so much that He knows how many hairs are on our heads.
- Ephesians 2:10 calls us His workmanship—made by Him. Anytime you believe something about yourself that's negative, you believe that about what God has created.
- 1 Peter 2:9 says we are chosen, royal, holy, and God's special possession.
- 1 John 3:1 calls us children of God.

Remember these truths when the Enemy comes at you with lies. Recall that we learned that he is like a roaring lion, prowling around, ready to take you down with lies.

No more. We will no longer listen to lies that make us believe we are inadequate. Doing so will take work. Returning to Romans 8, we learn that "those who live according to the flesh set their minds on the things of the flesh, but those who live according to the Spirit set their minds on the things of the Spirit. For to set the mind on the flesh is death, but to set the mind on the Spirit is life and peace" (vv. 5–6). What do you set your mind on? Things of the flesh and this world or things of the Spirit? If you aren't sure, you can reverse it a little. Do your thoughts bring life and peace, which is what is promised when we set our mind on the Spirit? If not, then you must change the way you think.

Going further into Romans, Paul taught, "Do not be conformed to this world, but be transformed by the renewal of your mind, that by testing you may discern what is the will of God, what is good and acceptable and perfect" (12:2). We stop pursuing things of the flesh when we stop conforming to this world. Instead, we work to be transformed, which can only happen when we hit reset on how we've been thinking. I had to stop believing I was inadequate and embrace my new name. This isn't easy or instant, but it is possible—just ask the Father to show you who you really are.

You might feel inadequate, but God says you are Wanda . . . I mean, worthy!

Pray

Father, I confess I have believed I am inadequate for too long. I have listened to the lies others have thrown against me for too long. But I'm no longer choosing to listen to those lies. [Go back to that list you wrote earlier and write "Lies" on top of that list.] Lord, I proclaim that all those things spoken about me are lies. In You there is no condemnation, so I do not receive that condemnation from others. Lord, I confess that I have thrown many stones against myself. Forgive me for believing those lies. [Go back to that list you wrote of stones you throw, and write "Lies" over them.] Father, I ask that You would transform my thinking. Show me what You say of me; help me to see myself as You see me.

Process

1. Of all the stones or lies that have been said about you, which ones have stung or stuck the most?
2. Do you need to remove any people from your life or set up better boundaries because of the harsh words they speak over you? (Putting up boundaries and removing hurtful people from your life doesn't make you a bad Christian; it makes you wise.)
3. Can you add other verses to the list that proclaim how God

sees you? Feel free to use the internet, Bible study tools, and friends to continue building this list of what's true about you.

4. How does hearing that God calls you *worthy* make you feel? Do you struggle to believe this? If so, why do you think that's hard to believe?

Hearers & Doers Challenge

I'm asking you to do that same kooky thing I did: give yourself a new name. As you look at the list of lies you wrote about yourself, that others have said and you have said, ask the Father for a new name. You can often know it's God speaking to you when it sounds too good to be true, or like something you'd never say about yourself. (That's how I knew Wanda was from Him. I would never in a thousand years have thought to call myself that.)

If you feel uncomfortable doing this, you won't be alone. Erin, who is like a sister to me, and I have gone to this retreat together a couple of times, and each time it's super awkward even to acknowledge the new name. Erin is so refreshing to be around because she is no-nonsense and incredibly intentional. But like most women, she struggles to see how amazing she is. I asked her if I could share two of her "name changes" with you to give you more examples. One year she went in feeling like she wasn't valuable. She had put this lie of a label on every area of her life. Then God gave her a new name: Ruby. If you knew Erin, you would laugh at this name. She isn't fancy at all. She'd much rather hang out in workout clothes or outdoors than dress up fancy. That's how she knew this was from God—she was more precious than rubies (Proverbs 3:15 NIV). Another year, she identified her core lie as being not enough if she didn't do all the things expected of her. One of the most beautiful things about Erin is how she demonstrates her love for others by serving them. But she realized she'd gotten caught up in *doing* and was finding her worth in that. That year the Lord gave her a new name: Carefree. As someone who cannot handle not doing something and also as someone who has fought hard to battle anxiety, she felt this name seemed misplaced. *That* is how you know! If it sounds too good to be true, or if it's a name you'd never come up with on your own, it's likely from the Father. It's okay if it doesn't come right away, so take a little time if you sense God is giving you a new name.

Write your new name here:

X_____

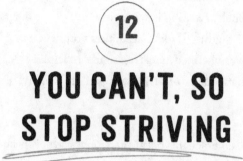

YOU CAN'T, SO STOP STRIVING

> You're off to Great Places! Today is your day! Your
> mountain is waiting, so . . . get on your way!
> **Dr. Seuss,** *Oh, the Places You'll Go!*

We've covered a lot so far, haven't we? We've looked back to identify failures, lies, and all the other things that have been holding us back. (Fair warning: Those aren't one-and-done practices. I come back to those approaches I taught you all the time. We must intentionally and continually choose to do so if we want to live abundantly.)

We've identified ways we've felt and started taking steps to think differently. Romans 12:2 says, "Do not be conformed to this world, but be transformed by the renewal of your mind, that by testing you may discern what is the will of God, what is good and acceptable and perfect." The only way to think differently than the world is by living a transformed, or changed, life. To live a changed life, we must renew our minds, which is how we find God's will. We trade old beliefs for new ones:

You feel exhausted, *but God* makes you strong!
You feel stagnant, *but God* has a purpose for you!
You feel lonely, *but God* is with you!
You feel disqualified, *but God* makes you new!
You feel overwhelmed, *but God* sends a Helper!
You feel inadequate, *but God* says you are worthy!

To help you embrace this belief, mark up those beliefs above.
Cross out how you've felt and underline "but God."
Example: ~~You feel exhausted~~, <u>but God</u> makes you strong!

I pray that you feel more hope for what's to come in your life as you continue to cross off those heavy feelings. This isn't to say that your feelings aren't valid or even justified, and it's also not to say they aren't true in some capacity, *but God can* still bring about abundant life from all you are feeling and have experienced. He isn't afraid of all those feelings or thoughts. They don't scare Him away, nor do they disappoint Him. He sees you, knows you, and has great things for you.

If you are anything like me, you see that list, know all we've worked through, and say to yourself, *But I still feel exhausted, stagnant or stuck, lonely or alone, hopeless, disqualified, overwhelmed, and inadequate.* I get that, because we often see where we think we should be, which rarely compares to where we are today.

Friends bought a house down the street from us a year ago and still haven't moved in. They bought it knowing they'd have to make many changes, and it's taking time, a lot of time. What they've gone through is similar to the journey we've been on together. The start of their renovation was similar to our initial gutting—pretty much everything but the studs had to go. One of their kids cried when he saw the house gutted and said, "What did you do to our house? You ruined our house!" I relate to him, don't you? Tearing things apart can feel like it's making more of a mess than helping. We've done quite the demo job on our lives by identifying what's broken and what doesn't belong. While HGTV can make demo day look like it happens in five minutes and is so much fun, we all know that's not reality. Demo takes time and intentionality, and it is really hard work.

Just like we've had to correct some of our thoughts and feelings under the surface, our friends had to replace everything behind those walls: the electricity, the air-conditioning, the water pipes, and more. Many things, while working fine, weren't up to current codes and needed to be fixed. We get it—while things seemed to work fine before, we know better now. So we've done similar work, resetting many unseen things in our minds and hearts. Each of these updates, while unseen at first, dramatically affects how we operate our lives.

As our friends move into the next phase, their house is starting to look more and more livable. Every time we walk through it, we see something new—molding, paint, tile, windows, cabinets, doors, and light fixtures! It's finally feeling and looking like a home. I hope you are seeing, in your own life, that you are coming along too. Be patient with your process. Just this past week, as our friends' contractor was prepping to lay the new floors, he found some spots in the subfloor that had to be corrected before he could move ahead. Similarly, in our lives, setbacks aren't always closed doors or proof that God can't. It might mean we are going to have to persevere. Two steps forward, one step back is still progress. We all have to be patient because the fun and pretty parts take time too. It will all be worth it very soon, I promise.

Impatience is a major struggle. Most of us aren't great at waiting. I'd do anything to have our besties eight doors down right now, and they are beyond ready to move in. Just last week I talked to my friend Kelley about some final decisions she has to make for the house. She is so done with the renovation and ready to move in. I encouraged her to be as intentional with these final steps as they were with the first ones. Sure, at the end of the day, it's just paint, wallpaper, and door handles, which don't matter much in the big scheme of things. I reminded her to stay patient with the process. It may feel like two steps forward and one step back, but they get closer each day. In our lives, progress can be hard to see when we feel stuck in the weeds doing the work. So let's pause and look up for a moment. I want you to see how far you've come in your journey.

Take a moment and reflect: Can you sense any progress in your "renovation" as you begin processing and applying what you are learning?

When you feel exhausted and totally spent, let hope rise as you sense God strengthening you.

Be intentional about noticing every time you don't stay stuck or stagnant but step into God's purpose.

Even when you feel lonely or alone, pat yourself on the back each time you choose to see God with you.

Celebrate every time you notice that you seek God for comfort instead of letting hopelessness fester.

Be proud when you start to disqualify yourself but instead allow God to make you new.

Revel in the relief you experience when you feel overwhelmed but trust the Helper and the help God gives you.

Give yourself a high five when you start thinking that you're inadequate but then switch to thoughts of your worthiness.

Before we move forward, we must acknowledge something essential: on our own, we can't. We can't fix our marriage, we can't change our diagnosis, and we can't concoct a purpose-filled life. We can't all of a sudden have deep friendships. Yes, we could try, and yes, we could even make some progress. But we aren't God, so why, when we could have the Creator of the universe leading the way, would we dare try on our own? We can't, *but God can*! We don't have to pretend or strive any longer to have what it takes. This is good news, so let's stop trying to avoid it.

We've looked at some of the words of the prophet Jeremiah already. As we turn to his words again, I pray that they will be seared into your heart so that you never forget them. Prophets had a hard life. While priests were often esteemed in society and people were drawn to them, prophets didn't receive such respect. Nearly every generation had a prophet who heard from God and spoke His words to the people. They were pivotal messengers, reminding people of God's ability and urging them to repent when they were too self-reliant. Jeremiah had tried hard to get the people to turn from their own ways and instead turn to God, but they continued to ignore him. They had grown comfortable in their promised land and didn't feel like they needed God anymore. They stopped listening to His voice and stopped following His commandments. They set up idols in the temple of God and built high places, sites of worship for other gods.

This may seem hard to relate to because we don't have idols or high places. However, we have our own modern-day versions. Idols are anything that we give greater attention to than God. To determine if I have any modern-day idols in my life, I ask myself, *If someone from a different day (like Jesus' day) were to observe my life, what or who would they say I worship?* They for sure would say my phone is an idol; how many hours a week do I spend staring at it? TV, especially if there's a great new series to binge. My kids and all their activities, evidenced by the number of hours I spend shuttling them around or sitting on the sidelines.

> What about you? What would be modern-day idols or high places for you?

I'm not saying all those things are bad. Phones are essential to life in this modern day, but surely there's a way to have them without them being all-consuming. I won't stop shuttling my kids around, but I need to pause and determine if their activites are too much. I'm not saying to throw your TV in the trash tomorrow. I'm simply saying to not get so absorbed by programming that we get lured into idolatry. Let's periodically ask ourselves if something has captured our attention and pulled us away from the Lord.

Jeremiah prayed, "Ah, Lord God! It is you who have made the heavens and the earth by your great power and by your outstretched arm! Nothing is too hard for you" (32:17). What a needed reminder. God created all that's in the heavens and all that's on the earth. Why would we settle for thinking we could do better with our lives? The Lord affirmed Jeremiah's assessment of Him, saying, "Behold, I am the LORD. . . . Is anything too hard for me?" (v. 27). Nothing is too hard for God, whatever you are facing or whatever you are hoping for.

We can trust God to do what only He can do. But we also have to acknowledge that we can't. And when we've pushed our way, we also need to repent—to confess to the Father where we got off the path and turn back to follow Him. "The Lord is not slow to fulfill his promise as some count slowness, but is patient toward you, not wishing that any should perish, but that all should reach repentance" (2 Peter 3:9). The Lord's timing can be so very frustrating, but often the slowness is actually a reflection of His patience with us. It's in His character to set all things up for repentance so redemption is possible for all. He doesn't want a single person to perish. Do you know the opposite of the word *perish*? It's *revive*, to bring back to life. That's what the Lord wants to do in your life, my friend. He is patient with you to turn to Him, to acknowledge that you can't make it on your own as you lay down your idols and leave your high places. Let Him resurrect what was once dead and bring about new and abundant life in you.

Pray

Usually, I give you a prayer to say, but this time I want to pray over you.

Father, thank You for bringing my friend this far. I pray that You will seal all Your work in her heart and soul! I beg, Lord, that You would protect her time when she sits to read. Please limit distractions or give her focus through the distractions. Teach her new ways. Correct ways or patterns that have been off. Encourage her to do the things she knows she needs to do. Draw her closer and closer to You. Show her how to love You, herself, and others! Teach her how to pray—You say to pray continuously; would you show her how? Help her to have faith, dream big, and still be realistic. What a tricky tension we walk with the line between faith and reality. Show her how both can exist! Show her when to wait, when to take baby steps, and when it's time to take a giant leap of faith! Give her clarity for when she needs to do things alone and when she needs to link arms with others. And as she wraps up the final pages of this book, would You give her confidence that she can and will stay free and live a more abundant life than she's ever known? Not abundance in possessions, but abundance in Your presence and purpose. Thank You. Amen.

Process

1. Which do you resonate with the most from the earlier list of ways you feel (exhausted, stagnant, lonely, disqualified, overwhelmed, and inadequate)?
2. Have you experienced God already beginning to transform your mind by changing how you think and feel?
3. How did it feel to admit that you can't? Was admitting that easy or hard? Why do you think it was that way for you?
4. What is a modern-day idol in your life? How are modern-day idols trickier to identify than idols in biblical times?

Hearers & Doers Challenge

I once taught a Bible study on idols and wanted to drive home the point that we can easily see how Bible-times statues of idols weren't good but can't as easily identify our modern-day idols. Now that you've identified a modern-day idol for yourself, make a physical version of it. When I taught that study, I gave everyone Play-Doh to form whatever their idol was. Then I challenged them to leave that representation in a place where they would see it often. Now it's your turn. Head to the store and grab a can of Play-Doh, or get some from the stash of your kids or a friend's kids. If you can't get your hands on Play-Doh, print off a picture that represents that item and put it up where you'll see it often.

PART 3

FINDING YOUR WAY IN THE WILDERNESS

As we move forward, fight the urge to look back; we've already processed the past and where we've been. Be honest with yourself and others as you accept that you aren't totally there yet, which is more than fine. Give yourself grace as you press on. Let go of checklists, let go of standards of perfection, and let go of all the "shoulds" you and others place on your shoulders.

The apostle Paul was arguably one of the most influential people in all of Christianity, and if he was humble enough to acknowledge he hadn't arrived at perfection (Philippians 3:12–13), we can acknowledge that in ourselves as well. This doesn't hold us back, but it gives us the confidence and security to "press on." Keep going—both through this book and with implementing the *But God Can* belief into your life.

For all the fellow skeptics who think, *Yeah, these are all nice ideas, but how do I actually live out all of this?* this is for you. This is the how. Are you ready to launch into experiencing the *But God Can* life that's truly abundant—more and better than you could possibly fathom? Let's go!

FIRST: LOVE GOD

Keep the joy of loving God in your heart and
share this joy with all you meet.
Mother Teresa

Religious leaders often tried to trap Jesus into saying something that would give them grounds to punish Him. On one occasion, a scribe stepped up and asked Jesus a question. We don't know this scribe's intent, if he was trying to trick Jesus or genuinely wanted to know the answer. Mark 12:28–30 says, "One of the scribes came up and heard them disputing with one another, and seeing that he answered them well, asked him, 'Which commandment is the most important of all?' Jesus answered, 'The most important is, "Hear, O Israel: The Lord our God, the Lord is one. And you shall love the Lord your God with all your heart and with all your soul and with all your mind and with all your strength."'" Thankfully for us, the answer wasn't contingent on intent. This man asked Jesus, of all the rules, which one was the most important. Jesus was clear:

love God. That's it; the most important rule of all the rules was simply to love God.

For Jews, this was a valid question. Flip through the Old Testament, and it won't take long to feel the weight of the many rules and the protocols for responding if you broke one. Jews had to keep an inordinate number of expectations at the forefront of their minds. In our tolerance-focused society, we can't fathom this. Today's culture struggles to feel the need for a Savior because we don't feel we need to be rescued. We aren't desperate for someone else to pay the price, carry the weight, or make a way when there seems to be no way.

One of my favorite things to do is teach God's Word. My weekends often include going to women's events, retreats, and conferences. But my absolute favorite place in all the world to teach is in women's prisons. The first time I went, I was terrified. I was seven months pregnant with our first daughter, and I'd watched one too many episodes of *Law and Order* growing up to know that this could go wrong. Having to sign paperwork in advance releasing the prison from liability if a hostage situation or something like that took place didn't help. I seriously debated not going. I'm so glad I made a promise to the Lord never to say no out of fear. I signed that form and walked into those gates the next week. I remember standing at the door to greet women as they filed into the room. It was so different from when I stood at the door at the weekly Bible study I taught at our church. These women's handshakes were limp and their eyes downcast. I always pray before I teach that God will let me feel the weight the women in the room are carrying, and that day felt nearly suffocating.

Then something happened as we prayed, sang, and journeyed through God's Word together. What I witnessed as God's Word was spoken and His truth proclaimed was unlike anything I've ever experienced. Those downcast eyes began to lift, and a spark was lit in them. You could tangibly feel the weight begin to lift off the women. We had both come timid, uncertain, and untrusting. But by the end, we embraced and wept and trusted God in ways none of us had before.

What is so breathtakingly beautiful about ministering in a prison is that these women understand their need for a Savior. These inmates are separated from society until the price for their sins has been paid. They know they need rescuing, and redemption is the most beautiful thing to witness once it clicks for them. They are locked away and told to get their act together. A new set of rules and expectations has been placed on their shoulders to clean up their lives. And then we come in with the Word of God, and our message isn't that they should stop that or do this; the message is that the most important thing they need to do is love God. That's it. Many of these women have been abused and used their entire life. They break as they learn that Jesus isn't trying to fix them, nor does He want them to follow another checklist in order to improve. All He wants is for them to love Him. He knows that when we fix our intent on loving Him, all the other things fall into place. He doesn't want us to be like the Jews who had to be focused on keeping the law—He came to free us from that.

Perhaps you've done a read-through-the-Bible plan before. I love them for many reasons, but I struggle at certain points. I especially want to skip or skim when we are in the early Old Testament and going over alllllllll the rules (yes, the multiple *l*s are needed). This part of the Bible is harder and harder for our culture to understand because the common practices of that day are not the common practices of today. It's also why it's harder and harder for people to understand how essential it was for Jesus to die for us. We live in a society where tolerance and acceptance are the mantras—do whatever feels right for you! But in biblical times the expectation was the keeping of *all* the laws, and for each thing done wrong, a sacrifice had to be offered to make it right.

The religious leaders who surrounded Jesus that day knew and followed all the laws to the letter. We who are immersed in Christian culture sometimes do the same. We focus on the rules because they are easy to track and measure. Love is immeasurable, and God is intangible, which makes loving God tricky to figure out. Aiming to live a good life is much easier, which is what most in our culture aim for, even those who identify as Christian. But living a good life isn't good enough; God wants an abundant life for you (John 10:10). We've already learned the thing that keeps us from life is the thief, Satan, who comes to steal, kill, and destroy. Abundance—an overflowing life—is what Jesus offers. The first step toward that is simply choosing to love Him, and loving Him is enough.

Jesus added a specific way to love Him: "with all your heart and with all your soul and with all your mind and with all your strength" (Mark 12:30). I could spend this chapter reviewing the Greek translations of *heart, soul, mind,* and *strength* so we know how to love God. Doing so, however, might give us another checklist of how to be or what to do. Together those things mean something simple, and it's found in the word before each of those other words: *all.* We are called to love God with *all* of ourselves. With every part of your body and life, choose to love God. We don't need to break down the words to the original language because there wasn't a part of our life that Jesus left out. God wants you to love Him with absolutely all you are and have.

This command to love God with our all might feel arbitrary, but it would have caused Jesus' listeners to recall Deuteronomy 6:5, where we first hear the phrase, "You shall love the LORD your God with all your heart and with all your soul and with all your might." In this chapter, Moses recapped some of the rules for the people before they were to go into their promised land. What's interesting, though, is that in Deuteronomy it wasn't identified as the greatest commandment. Sure, the header over this section in our Bibles may say "The Greatest Commandment," but that is hindsight placement by editors, not something that was actually stated. Jesus took all those rules and consolidated them into the most important: love God.

> In what specific ways could you aim to love God with your all?
> Where might you not be loving Him or just loving Him in part?

When God first told His people to love Him with every part of themselves, He also said they needed to remind themselves to do so, to practice the words of the law, and to teach His words on all occasions. I hope it encourages you to know that truly living out loving God with our all is not innate. Like any other love, it has to be learned and lived out.

Marriage has been a great teacher for me that love has to be grown, learned, nurtured, and pruned. I love my husband, but I don't always feel in love with him. Sure, in the beginning, it was relatively easy because I was caught up in the butterflies of our new relationship. Then life started to happen—bills, pressures, jobs, exhaustion, messes, children, and a thousand other things that are part of life. Sometimes I didn't love Chris as best I could because I'm human. Sometimes we needed counselors, mentors, or books to help us. Just as we must be intentional in loving our spouses, we must also be intentional in loving God with *all* we are.

Even as much as we try to love someone, we can still get it wrong. We see this modeled through the life of Peter. I love his audacity and fearlessness, and his indecisiveness is relatably endearing. In John 13:36–38, Peter proclaimed to Jesus that he would follow Him anywhere, even die for Him. Jesus replied to this great proclamation of love, saying, "The rooster will not crow till you have denied me three times." Then just as Jesus predicted, the rooster crowed before sunrise after Peter had denied Jesus three times. John 18:15 tells us that Peter did, in fact, follow Jesus after His arrest, only it was more of a lingering in the shadows than the kind of following he had previously done. When he was recognized as one of Jesus' disciples by the light of the fire where he was warming himself, he denied knowing Jesus. The thing he said he'd never do, he did. Can you relate to wanting so badly to love God with your all and yet feeling like you got it all wrong?

But God . . . That is not where this story, or yours, ends.

In John 20, Mary Magdalene went to Jesus' tomb and discovered that the stone had been rolled away. She ran to tell Peter and "the disciple whom Jesus loved" (John, the author; I love his confidence in being loved by Jesus). Peter and John ran as fast as they could to the tomb; and John lets us know he got there first but didn't go in. When Peter arrived, he didn't stay in the doorway like John; he went through it and was the first to witness that Jesus was no longer in the tomb. Over the course of days and weeks, Jesus appeared to many individuals and groups, proving that He had, in fact, risen from the dead. But Jesus knew one relationship needed to be further restored.

One day (it was likely the middle of the night), Peter went fishing with some of the other disciples. But it was one of those days when nothing happened. Despite their best efforts, they'd caught nothing. Then a man on the shore called out to them and asked if they had any fish. When they said no, he said to cast the net to the right side of the boat, and they were "not able to haul it in, because of the quantity of fish" (John 21:6). At that moment, John knew the man was Jesus and declared it. Peter must have had flashbacks to when Jesus first called him, and the same thing had happened—no fish caught all night until Jesus said to cast the net to the other side (Luke 5:1–11). And then he leapt into the water and swam to shore. I wonder if he flashed back again to when he attempted walking on water with Jesus (Matthew 14:22–33). Since it's not recorded that Peter walked on water again, we can assume it took him a while to get to land since he was a hundred yards away. That's Peter—don't think it through, just leap in faith toward Jesus, even if it means you are swimming the length of an entire football field. Yet another flashback surely crossed his mind as he approached Jesus. Jesus had made a charcoal fire, and surely Peter's senses brought him back to the last recorded fire when he had done what he said he'd never do: deny Jesus.

Senses have a way of bringing us back to a moment, don't they? A perfume or cologne reminds us of a person. The smell of a building brings you back to another place. The aroma of a meal brings back memories. A few years ago, when I was going through a particularly challenging season, a mentor of mine told me, "Jesus wants to redeem and restore all of it. Will you let Him?" He loves you so much that he wants every bit of you to feel it, all the way down to your senses. After they'd eaten, Jesus turned to Peter and asked, through the smoke of the fire, three times "Do you love me?" And three times Peter said, "Yes, Lord; you know that I love you" (John 21:15–17). Three denials, three questions, and three declarations of love. Jesus allowed Peter to redeem each denial with love.

Throughout this conversation and after, Jesus also gave Peter three ways he could show his love for Him: "Feed my lambs" (John 21:15), "Tend my sheep" (v. 16), and "Feed my sheep" (v. 17). Then, after all of this, he simply said, "Follow me" (v. 19). Peter's call hadn't changed since the first encounter with Jesus; all Jesus wanted was for Peter to follow Him. When Jesus proclaimed that the most important thing was to love Him with all our heart, soul, mind, and strength, He was simply saying, *I want all of you.* When He said to follow Him, He simply meant, *I want all of you and all you do.*

So how do we love God? It's not a checklist thing; it's a following thing. Loving and following Jesus takes time. Just like marriage, it will ebb and flow. Just like marriage, it will sometimes feel like you're on a mountaintop; other times, it will feel like you are miles apart. Like marriage, you will learn better ways to love God more over time. And just like marriage, you will learn what holds you back from loving God and try to eliminate those things.

Each of us will express our love for God differently. There's not one right and wrong way to love God. I can't give you a list of "Five Ways to Love God Better." Ask the Father to show you, then be intentional to really love Him with your all. As you go through the highs and lows of love, my hope for you is that you remember that Jesus always wants to be close to you. He will always find a way to restore what feels off. Come closer to the fire, warm yourself, and take it in.

Pray

Father, teach me to love You with all that I am. Forgive me for all the times that, like Peter, I've denied You. Forgive me for the times I was scared to love You, hesitant to love You, or too stubborn to love You. Show me how to love You with all my heart, soul, mind, and strength. Sometimes I feel like I'm faking it until I make it, or I'm clueless. I want You to know that I want to run to You like Peter—I want to leap out of the boat too! Show me how. Show me what it means to feed and tend to Your sheep. And show me how to follow You. I love You. In Jesus' name, I pray. Amen.

Process

1. Does it surprise you to hear that the most important rule is to love God and not something about being a good person? (Many of you have heard this before, but try to step back as if you are hearing it for the first time.)

2. How do you deny Jesus? Can you recall a time or way that you have denied Jesus? Like Peter, we often wouldn't think that we would, but there have been many times we have and still do.

3. Is there anything that has helped you love God? What changes do you need to make in your life to help you love God with your all?

4. If loving God means following Him, what does that look like for you? How are you not following God right now, and how could you follow Him?

Hearers & Doers Challenge

Write on a piece of paper any of the things you felt you've done that have denied God. Then, if possible, burn that paper. (Only do this if you can do so safely.) As it is burning, think about Jesus around that fire and how He welcomed Peter into a restored relationship with Him. Then write a list of things you love about God on a fresh sheet of paper: "I love You because. . ." Fold that list up and keep it in this book or put it somewhere special.

14

SECOND: LOVE YOURSELF

Beauty begins the moment you decide to be yourself.
Coco Chanel

Let me start off by admitting that I'm willing to be wrong in my interpretation of the Greatest Commandments. I learned that the Greatest Commandment is to love God, and the second greatest is to love others. "Love God and love others," we often hear. But we're missing a significant part. Even though our culture is rather self-centric, we've somehow neglected the part about loving ourselves. In fact, if I'm interpreting the second greatest command correctly, it says that the extent to which we love ourselves is how we are to love our neighbors (Mark 12:30–31).

This part has been passed over because it's hard for Christians to accept. I'm struggling with this myself because this self-love concept feels rebellious against what we are taught. Self-love, self-care, and self-compassion feel off-limits or wrong; there's too much self-focus. Aren't we supposed to be selfless? To think a different way feels too

BUT GOD CAN

far out of the lines that have been drawn for us, a boundary we must stand within. In reality, Jesus drew this line as a starting place. We can't really love others until we first start to love ourselves.

This is a truth I'm facing head-on right now, and it's hard to embrace. Let's look at Mark 12:29–31 in *The Message* to hear it a little differently: "Jesus said, 'The first in importance is, "Listen, Israel: The Lord your God is one; so love the Lord God with all your passion and prayer and intelligence and energy." And here is the second: "Love others as well as you love yourself." There is no other commandment that ranks with these.'" Don't you love how beautifully *The Message* translates the passage about loving God with all our heart, soul, mind, and strength? It also very clearly translates the next part, although the English Standard Version is worded a little differently: "The second is this: 'You shall love your neighbor as yourself.' There is no other commandment greater than these." So the second commandment has two commands folded within it: love yourself and others, but you will only be able to love others as well as you love yourself. This means self-love, self-care, and self-compassion aren't bad concepts brought to us by the self-help world. They are encouraged, actually commanded, concepts from the Father.

How can this be? Isn't Christianity all about dying to yourself? Absolutely! Dying to ourselves is how we are saved, but learning to love God, ourselves, and others is how we are sanctified. Loving yourself doesn't make you selfish. *Selfish* is defined as "concerned excessively or exclusively with oneself: seeking or concentrating on one's own advantage, pleasure, or well-being without regard for others."[1] People are selfish when they are overly concerned with themselves. Or when they are only focused on how something might benefit them. Philippians 2:3–4 actually affirms this interpretation. It is not telling you to forgo yourself for the good of others when it says, "Do nothing from selfish ambition or conceit, but in humility count others more significant than yourselves. Let each of you look not only to his own interests, but also to the interests of others." Yes, we are to be very aware of and concerned about others, but not at the sacrifice of ourselves. The verse doesn't say not to look to your own interests, only to look to the interests of others. Both Philippians and Matthew's gospel say that we are to love others just like we love ourselves and to look out for others just like we look out for ourselves.

So we need to ask ourselves whether we love or disregard ourselves. Anyone who loves themselves well gets a pass directly from this hard, self-love work because they are ready to focus on loving others. But if you are like 99.9 percent of women and struggle to love yourself well, this chapter is here to help you open up to this concept. Remember, I'm right there with you, struggling through the tension between what I've been taught and what I actually see in Scripture.

One of the top leaders in this concept of self-love, or self-compassion, is Dr. Kristen Neff. As one of the world's most influential research psychologists, she has written numerous books, studies, and articles on this topic. While neither she nor her work professes to be Christian, her scientific findings are confirmed by the words Jesus spoke two thousand years ago. The primary lesson I've learned from watching her videos on YouTube and reading articles she has published is that we need to stop self-judgment and start self-compassion. Stopping self-judgment is a familiar concept for us. We processed a lot of that as we addressed lies we believe at the beginning of this book. But starting self-compassion might sound strange or confusing. How do we choose to be compassionate toward ourselves? In all her work, Dr. Neff suggests responding to yourself as a trusted friend would respond to you.[2]

I'll share an example of self-judgmental thinking from my life. I could pretend this is hypothetical, but I'll just tell you that this is a normal day in the Kiser house, maybe not all in one day, but elements happen each day. I wake up early, typically before anyone else. But instead of making my coffee and opening my Bible to spend that hour journaling, praying, and studying Scripture, I check my email "real quick." Then somehow, my thumb automatically clicks to check social media and emails for an hour. I only realize it's been this long because my alarm goes off to get the girls up.

Enter the voice of self-judgment: *You are a terrible Christian! What a waste of a morning. Also, did you see so-and-so on Instagram? You are nothing like her! She prioritized spending time with God. You can see it right there in her picture with her Bible and the big takeaway she shared. Get your life together!*

Then one of my kids (or all three of them, depending on the day) wakes up in a mood. They refuse to get out of bed, I fix their hair wrong, and I'm the worst mom because I make them get their own breakfast and lunch together. Also, I look at them wrong and maybe breathe, which is also clearly unacceptable. In frustration, I snap at them; I raise my voice so much that my throat is sore.

Enter self-judgment: *You are a terrible mom! Did you see the look in your daughter's eyes when you yelled? She will never trust you now. And now you just showed her that yelling is how she should respond to you next time! What a terrible way to send your girls to school today!*

Then it's a cycle of mistakes: forget to put clothes in the dryer (*and now they will smell funny*); get on the Zoom call at the wrong time (*You might lose that client!*); go to Target for one thing and walk out with 38,753 things (*breaking the budget yet again*); and instead of eating kale, eat an unhealthy meal (*That's why you don't look like the other ladies*), and now you feel so tired (*Most women can juggle things; why can't you?*). That self-judgment voice is having a field day at every step of my day!

What voices of self-judgment do you often hear?

This could be every day or every so often. Go through a typical day and think through when self-judgment slips in. Maybe even record instances of self-judgment in a notebook or on your device as you go about your day.

My self-judgment voice is telling me that it was really, really dumb to be vulnerable. Telling you that I've done those things on a regular basis might cause you to disqualify me from helping guide you to *But God Can* living. Instead, I hope you hear that no one has it all together, certainly not me. I am a hot mess, *but God* loves me no matter what. We get to bring our messy selves to Him and let Him teach us how to love others as we learn to love ourselves.

I'm thinking about Jesus and how He told His mom and brothers that it wasn't time yet (He spoke up for Himself); how He often withdrew to be by Himself (He set aside alone time); He never apologized for being around sinners (He knew what and who He was called to); He didn't fight back when He was arrested (He knew what was true); He wept when His friend died (He allowed Himself to grieve); He allowed a woman to anoint Him with very costly perfume (He knew His worth); He slept (He rested when He needed to); He proclaimed that He was God's Son (He knew who He was and wasn't ashamed to admit it); and He made bold proclamations of healing (He knew what He could do). I could go on and on, but anytime you read the Gospels, start noticing how often Jesus loved Himself well.

If I could go back to my morning, instead of listening to the self-judgment voice in my head, I would ask the Holy Spirit to show me what is true. I'd implement self-compassion by trying to think with the voice of a trusted friend. I would look back at each of those experiences and say something totally different.

- **MORNING SCROLL:** *Oh, I totally get it; if I even look at my phone in the morning, I get stuck in some vortex for an hour. Give yourself a break! And maybe we could help hold each other accountable for not getting on our phones first thing in the morning. Tomorrow let's leave ours on the nightstand or counter until we've had some Jesus time.*
- **THEN, ALL THE CRAZINESS OF MY MORNING WITH THE KIDS:** *Parenting is so hard! We are basically holding our breath every morning, never knowing what kid we will get once they come downstairs. Yes, yelling isn't great, but we've all done it, so give yourself grace, send your kid a text apologizing, and maybe grab a treat after school to talk and make up. And have some hot chamomile tea—that usually helps my throat after a morning like that!*
- **CLOTHES IN THE DRYER:** *You aren't a terrible wife/mom/housekeeper; who hasn't done that? Just rewash them. It's no biggie! And think, now you don't have to put them away yet—that sounds like winning to me!*
- **TOO MANY THINGS AT TARGET:** *I can never go into Target and get just one thing. The other day I went to get one thing, and I walked out with a full cart only to get home and realize I didn't even get the one thing I needed!*

Are you catching on? It's going to feel really awkward at first, but the first and best way we can love ourselves is to change the way we think about ourselves. Before we wrap up this chapter, try that out.

Switch out your self-judgment for self-compassion.

Return to your list from the preceding reflection and write what a trusted friend might say to you if you told them what happened.

As an overthinker with high personal expectations, I find this process extremely challenging. As a life coach, I've observed that the self-help world is a slippery slope. This is not that. You will not find fake cheerleading from me to pump you up for just a moment, only to feel defeated when the emotion has worn off. I have zero interest in that. The whole self-help craze that teaches people only to see themselves as amazing falls flat when real life happens. We all know that fake-it-till-you-make-it mentalities are a joke; they work in the moment but never carry you through. Loving yourself isn't that. This is speaking to yourself the same way Christ would. It's returning to John 8 and defending yourself like Jesus defended the adulterous woman.

I did want to lead us back to another woman in Scripture who modeled self-love so well. She had every reason to linger in a state of self-pity and self-judgment, but instead, she chose to love herself really well.

Can you imagine bleeding nonstop for twelve years? The woman found in Mark 5:25–34 lived this reality. Even more disconcerting is that bleeding women were ceremonially unclean in these times. Women were already considered lesser in society and restricted to only one part of the temple. Since she was unclean for twelve years, this woman didn't even have access to that part of the temple, their version of church. To make matters worse, she was likely mortified every time she went in public because she was supposed to let anyone around her know she was ceremonially unclean so they didn't accidentally touch her and become unclean themselves. She hadn't stopped trying to get well all these years; she continued advocating for herself. She had gone from physician to physician; some took advantage of her, and the rest were unhelpful. She spent all she had and wasn't any better but had actually grown worse. And yet this woman didn't give up. She showed such tenacity by giving all she had and never giving up on herself. Can you think of where you were twelve years ago? Imagine in all that time that you were in physical pain, physically dirty, socially removed, and spiritually unclean. Also, imagine the roller coaster of hope at a new physician and disappointment when it didn't work out again—the shame and pain of being taken advantage of by some of them. But she loved herself so well that she never gave up.

She knew she had to put herself first to love herself well. She couldn't love others unless she cared for herself; she'd never be able to even get near others. Imagine all this time, all the failures, and she didn't lose hope for herself. She'd heard of this healer, but how many times had she heard of a healer, tried their method, and it had not worked out? She had nothing left because she'd spent all she had—she was out of options, except for this one now in front of her. Even after all she went through, she had so much hope. She believed, even after all she had tried, that if she simply touched the hem of Jesus' garment, she could be healed.

She was in the middle of the crowds, a place she wasn't used to; she reached out, and everything changed. We are told that she knew instantly that she was healed. After twelve years of feeling one way, everything changed in a moment of faith. Jesus knew something had happened, too, and turned to ask who had touched him. She came forward and shared her story with Him. And He replied to this woman who had loved herself so well and believed in Jesus so much, "Daughter, your faith has made you well, go in peace and be healed of your disease" (v. 34). He called her *daughter*. I don't know her familial connections, but we know from her uncleanness that she lived isolated and was looked down upon. And at this moment, she was called daughter. So tender, so endearing, so very much like Jesus.

The next time you reach out to help yourself, do it with the same faith as this woman. Don't hesitate, and don't let self-judgment slip in and tell you that loving yourself is selfish. After all, we can't love others well unless we first love ourselves well.

Pray

Typically, I write out a prayer for you. However, recently the Serenity Prayer was shared with me. I had heard the beginning part in movies and on TV shows. However, I'd never heard the full version until the other day. I thought this would be the perfect prayer to speak after reading this chapter. (You can also access this prayer online and tape it to your bathroom mirror, on your fridge, above your washer and dryer, or by any other place you frequent to focus on what is true about you throughout your day.)

> God, grant me the serenity to accept the things I cannot
> change,
> the courage to change the things I can,
> and the wisdom to know the difference.
> Living one day at a time, enjoying one moment at a time;
> accepting hardship as a pathway to peace;
> taking, as Jesus did, this sinful world as it is,
> not as I would have it;
> trusting that You will make all things right if I surrender
> to Your will;
> so that I may be reasonably happy in this life
> and supremely happy with You forever in the next.
> Amen.

—Reinhold Niebuhr[3]

Process

1. Do you struggle as I do with feeling that loving yourself is selfish? If yes, what do you think has contributed to that

mentality? If not, what do you think has helped you with this perspective?

2. What are your most common messages of self-judgment? Can you identify any triggers that cause them to pop up more than others?

3. How can you be more self-compassionate? In what ways or areas of your life do you need to work on this?

4. Like the hemorrhaging woman was persistent in her healing, is there something specific you need to do to love yourself well?

Hearers & Doers Challenge

This one will make you feel uncomfortable, but I pinkie promise it will be so good. Find thirty minutes to be alone. (This may be a challenge, so you may have to stay up late or wake up early.) Grab paper or a journal and something to write with, then sit or stand in front of a mirror. Now look at yourself, and for thirty minutes (you can set a timer) list all the things you love about yourself. Remember, when that voice in your head fights against this, shut it down. Ask yourself what God or a trusted friend might say about you. Write down those words.

15

THEN LOVE OTHERS

Love others so radically that they wonder why.
Unknown

She had trained for this moment her entire life. Hours and hours had been dedicated to this moment. Countless dollars for training, countless sponsorship dollars on the line. And so much of the world's eyes were locked on her. It was the summer of 2021, and the Olympics had been delayed an entire year. Simone Biles, considered the GOAT (Greatest of All Time) of gymnastics, was set to earn a record number of medals and even get a signature skill named after her. She did her practice run on the vault, and something seemed off. She was always remarkably steady. This time there was something different about her attempt. Moments later the entire international television audience watched her go to the sideline and talk to her coaches. She then put her sweats back on and exited the arena. A couple of days later we learned that she had what's called the "twisties"—a condition in which a gymnast's mind and body are no longer in sync. None of us can relate to the pressure she endured and the devastation she must have felt in letting down her country and her teammates. That would have been enough to make me curl up in bed and not want to face anything.

Do you recall what Simone did? She could have stayed in the locker room in frustration, embarrassment, disappointment, and anger at how things turned out. Since she's famous, she would have incurred judgment regardless of how she handled the situation. Most of us would have stayed in the locker room. Simone, however, came back out and cheered on her teammates. I remember watching her run up and down the sidelines, rushing to get them water or powder when needed. Simone chose to love herself well by taking herself out, and then she chose to love her teammates well by supporting them through the competition she'd trained her whole life for but didn't get to participate in. As a mom of three girls, I was grateful they could watch as she cheered her team on, even when dealing with her own stuff. What a lesson we could all learn from that moment.

This chapter will focus on what holds us back from loving others—and it's not because we don't know how to love. As Tom Rath's game-changing book *How Full Is Your Bucket* says, we simply can't pour out of an empty bucket.[1] We need to find ways to fill our buckets in order to pour out love to others. We could focus on the many hindrances to loving others well, but I've chosen the top five I've noticed in myself and others. I mention them in no particular order. And we will only scratch the surface of each; they could easily have their own chapter or even book. Nevertheless, they will provide a good starting place as you continue your *But God Can* journey.

Comparison and Envy

Another memorable Olympic moment for me was during the 2016 Rio Summer Olympics because it provided a great visual for the effects of comparison. Michael Phelps was swimming the 200-meter butterfly against Chad le Clos from South Africa and several other swimmers. In the 2012 Olympics, le Clos had beaten Phelps by just 0.05 seconds to secure the gold. This time, in the locker room before the race, you could see videos and pictures of Phelps totally focused and in the zone. He was unphased by le Clos, who was acting like a stereotypical middle school boy eager for attention. Phelps was having none of his antics. They dove into the water, and in the final lap, the moment I will never get out of my mind happened: Phelps was fully focused straight ahead, and le Clos turned to see where Phelps was. Le Clos lost by 0.7 seconds. One glance took him from being the defending Olympic gold medalist to not even making the podium. One glance at someone else took him out. This is what comparison can do to a person.

When we are so caught up in what's happening with others, we will find it impossible to love them.

In what ways can you see that comparison or envy affects your ability to love?
Share specific relationships or distractions that cause you to deal with comparison or envy.

As we can see in the Olympic story, looking at others out of envy only slows us down. The numerous verses in the Bible about envy aren't about restricting us but about revealing our hearts. One remedy for comparison is to actively love and show kindness to others. To celebrate with them even if it hurts. Turning comparison around is easy when we celebrate others well.

Here are a few verses to study what the Word says about comparison and envy:

- "A tranquil heart gives life to the flesh, but envy makes the bones rot" (Proverbs 14:30).
- "Not that we dare to classify or compare ourselves with some of those who are commending themselves. But when they measure themselves by one another and compare themselves with one another, they are without understanding" (2 Corinthians 10:12).
- "Let us not become conceited, provoking one another, envying one another" (Galatians 5:26).
- "Do nothing from selfish ambition or conceit, but in humility count others more significant than yourselves" (Philippians 2:3).
- "Where jealousy and selfish ambition exist, there will be disorder and every vile practice" (James 3:16).

Bad Boundaries and Unrealistic Expectations

Another thing that makes it impossible for us to love others well is if we don't set healthy boundaries with them. Most women struggle with boundaries, but I'd be willing to bet that Christian women struggle with them the most. We feel that relational boundaries are mean, exclusive, and in no way show love. This couldn't be further from the truth.

Some relationships require more boundaries than others. This isn't immature to acknowledge but wise. Certain relationships require distance for me to love the other person (and myself) well. I know that long stretches of time together will cause one or both of us to act in ways we would rather not. I also know that in some relationships, I have to set boundaries on how vulnerable I can be, what kind of access the person gets to the most personal parts of my story, heart, and life. Remember, not every person needs to be a good friend, nor does every family member need to be close. Jesus modeled this for us by His various relationship circles: crowds followed Him, His twelve disciples traveled with Him, but only three were in His inner circle. In addition, from what little we learn about His relationship with His family, they didn't really understand or support Him once He was living out His purpose as an adult.

With boundaries come realistic expectations. You cannot expect someone to be something they aren't.

For years I struggled with frustration and hurt from others' behaviors and choices. I wanted, prayed, and hoped they would be a certain way. Once, after a particularly hard session, my counselor asked me, "Becky, what would happen if you just expected X to continue behaving the way they always have?" Whoa. I don't know why I hadn't considered that before. I had been consumed with hoping and praying for that person to be how I knew they could be. Realistic expectations don't mean you lack hope or faith that things can change. This is a both-and process. We have realistic expectations for how they are (based on a pattern of behavior from the past), and we pray like crazy for things to change in full belief that, with God, all things are possible. We may not know how to love others well, *but God can* show us.

Here are a few verses to study what the Word says about bad boundaries and unrealistic expectations:

- "Keep your heart with all vigilance, for from it flow the springs of life" (Proverbs 4:23).
- "A soft answer turns away wrath, but a harsh word stirs up anger" (Proverbs 15:1).
- "Do not be deceived: 'Bad company ruins good morals'" (1 Corinthians 15:33).
- "Speaking the truth in love, we are to grow up in every way into him who is the head, into Christ" (Ephesians 4:15).

- "As for a person who stirs up division, after warning him once and then twice, have nothing more to do with him" (Titus 3:10).

Unforgiveness or Bitterness

Most of us have struggled with unforgiveness or bitterness at some point in our lives. And we've likely all heard that holding on to bitterness and unforgiveness hurts the one who holds it far more than it ever hurts the other person. I've watched that happen in my own life and in the lives of many others. We hold on to our bitterness because we feel justified in withholding forgiveness.

Forgiveness is not shoving feelings down and plastering on a smile and a definitive statement that you have forgiven the person. Too many Christians force forgiveness because they feel like they should forgive before the sun sets (Ephesians 4:26). I don't know if this is a good parenting choice or not—only time will tell—but when one of our girls does something hurtful to another, I require that she apologize, ask for forgiveness, and do what she can to make it right. But I never force the other to say, "It's okay. I forgive you."

I chose this policy because forgiveness is a choice that sometimes takes time. I never want my girls to become numb to the process. I don't want forgiveness to be mechanical for them, saying words they "should" but which their hearts never mean. I've seen too many Christian women hurting over suppressed unforgiveness. They've plastered the words "I've forgiven them" on a broken heart but have never really forgiven or dealt with their bitterness or hurt.

Do you have unresolved bitterness or unforgiveness in your heart?

Write the initials of those you need to forgive or the circumstances below. Ask God to help you forgive and to show you what that looks like.

Forgiveness is often not a one-and-done thing. Yes, dealing with the hurt of little things is usually simple. But multiple rounds of forgiveness may be necessary for more significant things. Often, just the thought or sight of something triggers the pain of a previous offense, and we must pause and pray again. As we work on forgiveness, bitterness often lessens and goes away.

When I was younger, I experienced trauma. The details don't matter here because we can all relate to ordeals from which the pain never fully disappears. I was in a season where this trauma had been triggered again, and I was struggling. My counselor wasn't afraid to push me to deal with this freshly resurfaced hurt. As we processed these memories and how they affected me, she said, "Becky, I don't think you've forgiven X. I think that's what you need to focus on this week."

I didn't want to. I wanted this person to feel as badly as I felt. But that made me feel even worse. So the next day, after I put baby Karis down for a nap, I sat on my couch to work on forgiveness.

Forgiveness isn't giving the offender an excuse or saying that what happened is okay. Forgiveness doesn't mean you are always happy and feeling blessed. Forgiveness is more than words uttered from your lips and much more about your heart releasing what has been weighing you down.

So I sat cross-legged on our tan corduroy couch with my hands held open in my lap. I spoke the words, "Lord, help me to forgive X." Then, in uncontrolled response, my lip quivered, my head nodded no, and tears streamed down my face. I remember speaking out loud, "No. No, I can't forgive this. It's unforgivable." And then a calling to forgive washed over me again. I spoke forgiveness over one memory after another. Forgiveness is taking the burden off your shoulders and sending it on its way.

Give yourself time and grace as you deal with unforgiveness. Don't push it down because when you let things fester, they cause much more hurt. Using the strategies I'm sharing will help you heal. I don't really believe that time heals all wounds, but I do believe that *God can* heal all wounds, physical and emotional. Instead of shoving things down or pushing through on your own, trust God to do the healing.

Here are a few verses to study what the Word says about unforgiveness or bitterness:

- "Hatred stirs up strife, but love covers all offenses" (Proverbs 10:12).
- "Whenever you stand praying, forgive, if you have anything against anyone, so that your Father also who is in heaven may forgive you your trespasses" (Mark 11:25–26).
- "Beloved, never avenge yourselves, but leave it to the wrath of God, for it is written, 'Vengeance is mine, I will repay, says the Lord'" (Romans 12:19).
- "Let all bitterness and wrath and anger and clamor and slander be put away from you, along with all malice" (Ephesians 4:31).
- "See to it that no one fails to obtain the grace of God; that no 'root of bitterness' springs up and causes trouble, and by it many become defiled" (Hebrews 12:15).

Gossip

Gossip is defined as a "rumor or report of an intimate nature; chatty talk."[2] It has become so normalized in our society that we all know we shouldn't do it but we do it anyway. We are in this struggle together. There is a fine and fuzzy line between talk and gossip. My litmus test for if my words are gossip is whether I'd say them if the subject of the conversation was present. I also ask if others' names are safe in my mouth? Can others trust that I speak well about them? The best way for others to trust if you are speaking well about them is if you are speaking well about others to them.

How has gossip negatively affected your relationships?
Take note of how it hurts you or others and how you feel after you've gossiped.

My encouragement for you, as it is often my advice to myself, is to own where you have gone wrong. Last year I got right in the middle of what I'd call a gossip storm involving one unfortunate event after another. I knew I should have pulled myself out of it, but I didn't. I still don't know why. In my adult life, I'd never made such poor decisions with the words I said and the words I listened to. My closest friends could tell you I have a strong line on not gossiping. There are always better things to talk about, and any conversation can pivot to a productive dialogue. Even so, that doesn't mean I don't ever get caught up in gossip.

After that gossip storm blew up, I had to make hard calls and own where I went wrong. One person who didn't know me well said, "I just don't trust you. Never have, never will." That comment still stings every time I see her. I've never in my life had anyone accuse me of being untrustworthy. That she got me so wrong hurts, but it's also my fault. Gossip hindered my ability to love her and the others in that situation because trust was breached. It was a much-needed lesson, even if it was a hard one. Not being careful with the words that I spoke hindered my ability to love others.

Here are a few verses to study what the Word says about gossip:

- "Set a guard, O LORD, over my mouth; keep watch over the door of my lips!" (Psalm 141:3).
- "Whoever goes about slandering reveals secrets; therefore do not associate with a simple babbler" (Proverbs 20:19).
- "Let no corrupting talk come out of your mouths, but only such as is good for building up, as fits the occasion, that it may give grace to those who hear" (Ephesians 4:29).
- "Besides that, they learn to be idlers, going about from house to house, and not only idlers, but also gossips and busybodies, saying what they should not" (1 Timothy 5:13).
- "If anyone thinks he is religious and does not bridle his tongue but deceives his heart, this person's religion is worthless" (James 1:26).

Selfishness

Last but certainly not least, simply being selfish is another significant thing that keeps us from loving others well. Selfishness is "a concern for one's own welfare or advantage at the expense of or in disregard of others: excessive interest in oneself."[3] Being concerned for yourself isn't wrong, but being excessively or exclusively concerned with oneself is. Showing yourself self-love or self-compassion is not selfish. Wanting to do well isn't wrong; being consumed with your own advantage or doing well while disregarding others is wrong. Do you see how there's a difference in the extremes?

At certain times, we could stand to be a bit more selfish, as we discussed in chapter 15. But that doesn't mean we should slip into the other extreme and default to selfishness.

Are there certain environments or relationships in which you bend toward selfishness?

Try to get as specific as possible here with what people or places trigger selfish tendencies.

Here are a few verses to study what the Word says about selfishness:

- "Incline my heart to your testimonies, and not to selfish gain" (Psalm 119:36).
- "Do not withhold good from those to whom it is due, when it is in your power to do it" (Proverbs 3:27).
- "Love one another with brotherly affection. Outdo one another in showing honor" (Romans 12:10).
- "Let no one seek his own good, but the good of his neighbor" (1 Corinthians 10:24).
- "Let each of you look not only to his own interests, but also to the interests of others" (Philippians 2:4).

Chris and I had looked at rings together, so I knew an engagement was coming. It was no longer a matter of *if* and totally a matter of *when*. My papaw always joked about us Smiths (my maiden name) that we (with his hands waving exasperatedly in the air) are "do everything right now" people. He wasn't wrong. Once I make up my mind and feel certain about something, I see no use in waiting for the inevitable.

I was ready to be Chris's wife and was getting tired of all the time it was taking for him to propose (you should also know that we'd been dating less than a year at this point, probably closer to eight months, so it's not like I'd been waiting long).

One day during a time of prayer and Bible study, I turned to the "love chapter" and read 1 Corinthians 13:4–7. As I read through each thing that defined love, I was convicted. So I called Chris and asked him to come over after work. I remember sitting on the floor in my living room and telling him, "I'm sorry I've not been very patient. I've wanted to rush this because I can't wait to be your wife. I haven't been kind to you when you've had to move plans around. I've envied others who are already engaged." I worked my way through each definition of love, apologizing to him for each thing I had gotten wrong.

Do you know what happened that very week? He proposed. All along, he was planning the engagement, which was beyond amazing, by the way. I learned the hard way that sometimes the best way to love others well is to fix where I'm not loving them well. I can do that by focusing on the biblical descriptions of love and implementing those things.

> Love never gives up.
> Love cares more for others than for self.
> Love doesn't want what it doesn't have.
> Love doesn't strut,
> Doesn't have a swelled head,
> Doesn't force itself on others,
> Isn't always "me first,"
> Doesn't fly off the handle,
> Doesn't keep score of the sins of others,
> Doesn't revel when others grovel,
> Takes pleasure in the flowering of truth,
> Puts up with anything,

Trusts God always,
Always looks for the best,
Never looks back,
But keeps going to the end.

—1 Corinthians 13:4–8 MSG

This isn't a checklist. This isn't something you pass or fail. It is a map to show us the way to love others. Just as I don't love Chris perfectly today, even a decade and a half into marriage, you won't love people perfectly after you finish this chapter. However, we will love people better—progress, not perfection—with a balance of grace and discipline.

Pray

Father, I confess that I haven't loved people as well as I could. Will You forgive me for comparing myself to others? I want to be a cheerleader for others, not envious of others! In challenging relationships, please show me how to set better boundaries. Help me to release any unforgiveness and bitterness I've shoved down deep. Give me the grace I need to forgive others truly—may it be genuine! Tame my mouth—I don't want to gossip; I want others' names to be safe in my mouth. Show me how to die to myself and put others before me. Help me to learn how to be selfless while loving myself well. Holy Spirit, would You guide me all throughout the day and show me how to love those around me specifically? Thank You. Amen.

Process

1. Identify who your others are. Who do you spend significant time around? Who do you encounter throughout your day?

2. Of the five areas listed, which area do you struggle with the most? What do you think you could do to choose to love proactively?

3. Think of three relationships in which you want to learn to love others well. Write out what you might do to love them well.

4. What are your favorite ways to show others you love them?

Hearers & Doers Challenge

Use your words: Think of one person right now and send that person a note sharing what you love about them. (This can be a text, email, or card in the mail.)

Use your time: Who can you do something for or spend time with to show them that you love them?

Bonus: If there's anyone you need to call and make things right with like I had to do, do that today. Send a text or email and ask if you can talk in person or on the phone.

16

WHERE DO YOU NEED A "BUT GOD CAN"?

Give me the Love that leads the way
The Faith that nothing can dismay
The Hope no disappointments tire
The Passion that'll burn like fire
Let me not sink to be a clod
Make me Thy fuel, Flame of God.

Amy Carmichael

We now have clarity on things Jesus said were most important: love God, ourselves, and others. That is our foundation. If it's off, everything we put on top will crumble. We can't move forward into *But God Can* living without a strong foundation. And I'll continue to say until you say it to yourself naturally: it is built with progress, not perfection.

When I was younger, my mom would pack up her little Plymouth

Horizon, and we would hit the road for weeks at a time. We drove all over the United States, even into Mexico and all the way up to Canada, and camped along the way. The car would be packed to the top, and somehow my brother and I squeezed in between all the camping supplies, clothes, and food. My mom would have her left leg in her seat because she had to keep a bag where her left foot would go. We would blast the same cassette tapes on our boom box for as long as the batteries would last. And to pass time, I read every single Baby-Sitters Club book ever written. By the midpoint of our road trip, we could set up camp in under five minutes. This is because sometimes we would pull into the campsite as the sun was about to set. About 95 percent of the time, our late arrival was because my mom had to take a "shortcut." This was before the days of GPS that recalculated your route for you; cell phones hadn't even been invented yet. Without fail, my mom would see a road that called to her for some reason. It might have been the county name on the sign, a field that looked too enticing to pass, or simple curiosity. She'd turn off our predetermined path and say, "Let's take a little shortcut." My brother and I would moan in unison because we knew this was not, in fact, a shortcut.

I equate this point in our journey to that experience. The past few chapters might have seemed like I was taking you on one of my mom's "shortcuts." However, it was an essential part of our trip, much like when our GPS apps today say, "Rerouting." What we've processed in the preceding chapters adds to the *But God Can* adventure you are embarking on. You've come a long way, further than you realize. We are pulling up to the Grand Canyon, witnessing all its colors, ridges, and valleys. We are climbing our way up the mountains of Canada, pulling on our sweatshirts because the temperature is dropping, and staying alert because moose may wander onto the highway. And we will likely have some adventures like my family had when we thought we were entering a hole-in-the-wall authentic Mexican restaurant, only to stumble into someone's house and wake an elderly man from his siesta. (I still wonder if his family tells stories about how a gringo family literally fell into his house. I can still hear my mom talking loudly as if that would help her English make sense to this suddenly awakened man. "I'm so sorry! Lo siento! I'm so sorry!") Some things we will get down quickly, like setting up our tent. And some things will hurt, like shutting my brother's hand in the trunk and being unable to find the keys to unlock the trunk, leaving his hand stuck for quite some time. (Still so sorry about that, bro.) We will do things we never imagined, like my brother did when we reached the Grand Canyon (that's a family secret, but I hope you make your own secrets on your adventure too). We will face our fears like we faced bears, snakes, and other unidentifiable things when we had to set up camp in the dark.

As a parent myself now, I can't get over my mom's courage to take us on those adventures. I barely feel comfortable running to the grocery store without my phone to provide a sense of security and control. So to pack up my kids, fill the car to the brim, and just set off feels a bit foolish and absolutely terrifying. But as I tell my girls when they beg to watch certain YouTube channels or ask when they can have social media like their friends, "I don't want you to waste your life watching others live theirs. Go live your life!"

The Bible gives the account of Abram (later Abraham), a man who stepped out in faith to embark upon a great adventure with God. "God told Abram: 'Leave your country, your family, and your father's home for a land that I will show you. I'll make you a great nation and bless you. I'll make you famous; you'll be a blessing. I'll bless those who bless you; those who curse you I'll curse. All the families of the Earth will be blessed through you.' So Abram left just as GOD said" (Genesis 12:1–4 MSG). As I am with my mom, I'm in awe that Abram would just go. He didn't have a clue where he was going, only that he should go. He had a promise that God would show him where to go and a promise that it would work out.

Abram thought he had a plan for his life, but God called him to go on a little "shortcut" that changed not just his life but all of our lives.

Friend, the same adventure is offered to you. Will you go? Will you pack up all you have, risk all you have, and leave all that feels secure so you, too, can experience a *But God Can* life?

I'm beyond excited about what will happen in your life as we continue. We've had to do a lot of mindset shifting to get to where we are right now. A lot of what we've covered are things you will need to continue referencing—progress, not perfection! As we continue on, remember:

~~You feel exhausted~~, *but God* makes you strong!
~~You feel stagnant~~, *but God* has a purpose for you!
~~You feel lonely~~, *but God* is with you!
~~You feel disqualified~~, *but God* makes you new!
~~You feel overwhelmed~~, *but God* sends a Helper!
~~You feel inadequate~~, *but God* says you are worthy!

And as we move forward, we do so by loving God with all we are, learning to love ourselves, and choosing to love others well. With this foundation, we will see God do a work that only He can do! You can't, *but God* most certainly *can*!

How do you need a "but God can" to happen in your life?
Be brave here! Be bold. What mountain are you up against? What sea are you stuck in front of? What seems absolutely impossible and overwhelming? Write it down below. Nothing is too small or too big.

In Matthew 14, we meet Jesus in the midst of more grief. Considering what you just shared, I hope you feel seen in whatever overwhelms you. Jesus had just learned that John the Baptist, His cousin, His friend, who baptized Him, had been beheaded. He sought to be alone and tried to pull away from others for a bit. But the crowds followed Him, and "he had compassion on them and healed their sick" (v. 14). Take note of Jesus' character: He always makes space for people; His heart bursts with compassion for *you*. Five thousand men, and that's not counting all the women and children, followed Jesus that day. I love a good act of faith, but I'm also an unrelenting planner (some might say a control freak). So I completely understand the disciples when they came up to Jesus as the sun was getting lower in the sky and said something like, "It's getting late, and this place doesn't have food or shelter. Let's send all these people on their way because they are about to get hangry" (my paraphrase). Jesus told them that the people didn't have to go away; the disciples just needed to feed them. They rebutted, "We have only five loaves here and two fish" (v. 17). The math wasn't adding up.

Nevertheless, Jesus told them to bring Him what they had. Then He used what was available to do a miracle. He fed the thousands with only the five loaves of bread and two fish they had. What might He do in your life if you stopped seeing only the five loaves of bread and two fish and started seeing what God could do with them?

Do you find yourself only able to see the five loaves of bread and two fish? How so?

As you consider all parts of your life, not just the ones that seem like mountains, ponder whether you might be settling. Sometimes we disguise a lack of faith to look like and even feel like contentment when it's not. Where might you be settling?

We learned that all five thousand-plus people were satisfied, and the disciples took up twelve baskets full of broken pieces left over. Did you catch the lesson? You don't have to know the details of how God will work your miracle. You don't have to understand how it's possible. All you need to do is bring God what you have and let Him work on your behalf. There wasn't any way those disciples could have fed those people independently. Their idea to send the people back into town for food wasn't bad or disobedient. That's all they could do on their own. *But God can* take what seems impossible and make all things possible. All He needs is for you to offer up all you have, even if it seems insufficient. Whatever it is that you are facing or will face, God is more than able. You can't, *but God* absolutely *can*!

For any of you skeptics, I will ask the obvious next question: "But what if He doesn't?" He might not. So keep praying and seeking what His plans are. You don't need to force your way; wait on God's way. You don't have to know how; you just need to wait on Him. You don't need to know where or when; you just need to take a baby step in the direction you sense Him leading. You don't even need to know if it will work out; just take a leap of faith and watch the Father do what only He can do. As we will see in the next few chapters, God doesn't work like a genie in a bottle. Not everything you surrender to Him will go as you hope. Not every "shortcut" will lead to a beautiful adventure. Sometimes the answer is no, and sometimes there are dead ends even on roads we are supposed to take.

I don't understand why God doesn't heal everyone from disease. I don't know why God doesn't restore every broken relationship. I don't know why everything we try doesn't succeed. Scripture shows us that God has a plan and purpose in every heartache, failure, pain, and detour. But often we can't readily see God's plan and purpose, and we struggle to put our trust in Him. Faith, however, is trusting what you cannot see. You don't know what's up ahead, *but God* does. On your own, you can't handle what's up ahead, *but God can*. In all these things, you can't, *but God* absolutely *can*!

Elijah, a prophet of God, was tired of the people going back and forth between worshiping God and Baal. He said, "How long will you go limping between two different opinions? If the LORD is God, follow him; but if Baal, then follow him" (1 Kings 18:21). They had to choose. How much can we relate? We trust God, but we also trust in ourselves and what is right in front of us. Those worshiping Baal had 450 prophets to carry out the task they were about to be given, but the Lord God had only Elijah to work with. The challenge was for a bull to be given to each group—those, including the 450 prophets, who worshiped Baal, and also those, just Elijah, who worshiped the Lord God. They would set up a sacrifice, laying a bull on wood but putting no fire to it. Each group would call upon their god to light the fire. Then they'd know whose god was the true God by whichever sacrifice was consumed. This was a bold and brave challenge Elijah was setting up. He was really putting his faith in God on the line.

Elijah gave the Baal prophets a head start, as if a group that size needed one. They prepared the sacrifice and then "called upon the name of Baal from morning until noon" (1 Kings 18:26). They grew weary and started limping around their altar. So they tried harder, crying out louder and even cutting themselves (as was a common custom). Even so, verse 29 says about their god, "There was no voice. No one answered; no one paid attention." Sound familiar? Have you done all you possibly could on your own, and there's been nothing, not a voice, an answer, or one tiny spark of fire?

On our own, we can't, *but God can*. Elijah set up his altar, placing a bull atop the wood, just as the Baal worshipers had done. However, as we see in verses 32–35 there was one difference: he built a trench around his altar. Then he did something that made absolutely no sense: he told the people to fill four jars with water and pour it on the offering and the wood. Even though he'd put the people's belief in God on the line, he decided to pour water all over what he was going to ask God to light with fire. Then he said, "Do it a second time." Then he said, "Do it a third time." There was so much water at this point that it ran around the altar and filled the trench.

But God can.

Elijah the prophet came near and said, 'O Lord, God of Abraham, Isaac, and Israel, let it be known this day that you are God in Israel, and that I am your servant, and that I have done all these things at your word. Answer me, O Lord, answer me, that this people may know that you, O Lord, are God, and that you have turned their hearts back.' Then the fire of the Lord fell and consumed the burnt offering and the wood and the stones and the dust, and licked up the water that was in the trench. (1 Kings 18:36–38)

But God can. The offering was drenched, the wood was soaked, and the moat was filled. Hundreds of the others who worshiped Baal had spent all day begging their god to send a spark to set their offering on fire. But our God, in answer to the simple prayer of one man, not only sent a spark but burned up everything instantly in an all-consuming fire.

But God can. What courage! What audacity! I can't imagine having this kind of faith, especially in front of hundreds of people. However, it's the very faith I want for myself and the very faith I want for you. What could God do if we took these things we are holding on to, doing everything in our might to change, and instead simply trusted God to do what was best? Knowing that sometimes God will burn everything up feels like starting over. Other times it feels like He has rained on our parade and literally poured something all over us so that we can't even see straight. Sometimes we think He answers too quickly; sometimes He doesn't answer at all. And sometimes His answer is nothing like we'd hoped or imagined.

One of the most comforting and slightly frustrating passages in the Bible is God speaking in Isaiah 55:8–11:

> For my thoughts are not your thoughts,
>
> neither are your ways my ways, declares the LORD.
>
> For as the heavens are higher than the earth,
>
> so are my ways higher than your ways
>
> and my thoughts than your thoughts.
>
> For as the rain and the snow come down from heaven
>
> and do not return there but water the earth,
>
> making it bring forth and sprout,
>
> giving seed to the sower and bread to the eater,
>
> so shall my word be that goes out from my mouth;
>
> it shall not return to me empty,
>
> but it shall accomplish that which I purpose,
>
> and shall succeed in the thing for which I sent it.

This verse is frustrating because it does confirm that sometimes, no matter how much you pray in faith, things can go a different way than you think best. The explanation for it, however, is very comforting: God's ways aren't our ways; His ways are higher. Further on in this chapter we read that God brings rain and snow down to water the earth and make things grow. From heaven, God "waters" whatever is happening in your life. He does what you can't do. You can't force something to happen, *but God can* sprout green life any minute from the darkness of your soil.

One way or another, God is crafting a story you couldn't even fathom, and you certainly couldn't concoct yourself. Let Him. Surrender to Him. His ways are higher, and His thoughts are higher. Don't settle anymore.

Pray

Father, help me to be brave like Elijah as I begin to trust You with the things I've listed, the things I wasn't ready to list, and all the unknown things to come. Help me to trust that You are more than able. But help me to bring what I have and to do what I can, knowing that when I live surrendered, You can multiply and bring growth where I couldn't. I'm asking You to work a miracle, a true "but God" moment, in my life.

Process

1. Do you want to live a grand adventure—a life more than your current life? If yes, how so? If not, why not?

2. How have you experienced God using a detour or dead end in your past? How might that encourage you in your present?

3. Pick at least one of the situations you listed above for which you need a "but God can" to happen. Write out all that you've already done on your own and/or all you can think of to do. Now, write out the best outcome that could come from those efforts. Consider how that compares to what you've read from Isaiah 55. Are you comfortable and looking for God to be your genie in a bottle, or are you living open handed and watching God do something beyond what you can think or imagine?

4. Of all the things you listed, where do you want a "but God" transformation to happen the most?

Hearers & Doers Challenge

In the next chapter, we will talk about what you can do now that you've identified the thing you want to see a "but God" moment to happen with. Until then, share with at least one person where you are asking God to do something big. You can ask them to pray, to hold you accountable—whatever you think you need.

(17)

PRAY AND DREAM

If your dreams don't scare you, they are too small.
Richard Branson

There are times we are going through all the motions of life but getting absolutely nowhere. Life is flying by in a whirlwind, passing by so quickly, but we are certain this isn't an abundant life. I've found that most women I meet or coach are one of these two things—prayers or dreamers. Those who feel really confident with prayer often feel bad dreaming, as if it's not trusting God. And those who are great dreamers often struggle with prayer because of its lack of doing, for lack of a better word. So my hope is that we'd find stability where we are already strong and grow in confidence in areas where we aren't strong. If you feel weak in both areas, then you are about to experience a strength you've never known.

Prayer means stopping our spinning on the hamster wheel; it takes a lot of faith to stop. Bowing our heads and opening our hands to the Father—literally or figuratively—is the most beautiful act of surrender. It slows us down and is our way of acknowledging that on our own we can do nothing; we need God!

Dreaming is when we look up and around and ask, "What could be?" and "What if?" A basic rule for any good brainstorm is "No idea is a bad idea." But before we dream, we pray.

[Pray] at all times in the Spirit, with all prayer and supplication. To that end, keep alert with all perseverance, making supplication for all the saints.

Ephesians 6:18

Prayer can be where many women get stuck, and many women skip past it. Some are so afraid to do the wrong thing that they keep praying and praying and "praying" about it. (The last one is in quotes because I think sometimes we even say we are praying about it, but we actually aren't; we are just straight-up avoiding it, totally hiding.)

Friend, I hope by now we know each other well enough that you know my heart on this—prayer is good, but let's not hide behind it any longer. Jesus in the garden of Gethsemane (Mark 14:32–42) prayed earnestly and repeatedly. But then He got up and faced things. It's the not knowing that keeps us praying most of the time. We don't want to fail; we don't know where to start. It seems scary; what if we go the wrong way? If this is your situation, get up and get going. It's time to stop hiding behind prayer.

Are your prayers less filled with faith and more like Moses arguing with God at the burning bush? Moses was begging for an out, looking for any other way but the way God had clearly laid before him. Moses had grown comfortable with how his life was, and even though God was saying He would do it all, Moses wasn't sure. I get that. Trusting God can be so very scary.

Now, the rest of us are so ready to leap that we skip prayer. Or we rush past it so quickly that it's more like, "Hey, God! So I'm doing this thing. Will you bless it? Thanks! Amen." I can speak from personal experience about this. It's not that you aren't following God's plan or even that you aren't in the Spirit as you go. However, you, too, will miss the "but God can" part of what you are doing because you are doing it in your own efforts. Sure, you might do something really great. *But God can* do something greater—He can multiply in ways you simply can't. So let's start asking Him!

This isn't a how-to section on prayer because there isn't a formula for prayer or a specific way to pray. Nevertheless, you can search online for ways to pray, ask friends and mentors, and read books on prayer. You'll find some great ways to get started, and you can then let that evolve into a conversation style that works for you.

Here are a few ways I talk to God (which is all prayer is):

- **ON THE GO.** The achiever in me had a hard time with this approach because it didn't feel reverent enough. I realized, however, that dialoguing with the Lord throughout my day builds a stronger relationship with Him. As things pop into my mind, I don't typically stop and pray; instead, I keep on and pray. Sometimes it's thanking God for something I noticed. Other times it's praying for people as they come to mind. It's a lot of processing decisions and next steps. You can do this out loud or in your head, whatever works for you.
- **P-R-A-Y.** When I first became a Christian, I was clueless. I had absolutely no idea where to start. Someone shared the acronym P-R-A-Y with me, and it has shaped a good portion of all my prayers.

- **PRAISE.** Spend time praising God for who He is. Sometimes I praise Him for things I saw Him do or a part of who He showed Himself to be in the Bible. Other times I praise Him for things that have happened or are happening in my life. Try to take note of where you see the Father moving around you. Taking time to praise God boosts your confidence and faith in Him as you seek to live abundantly. Being intentional to notice Him will shift your perspective.

- **REPENT.** Many of us forget about this step after becoming Christians. We don't like to focus on sin or wrong choices; we've already repented and fully turned to Jesus. However, I've found it freeing to thoughtfully and consistently repent. The practice of letting the Spirit have access to your heart, mind, and actions will lead you into more abundant living. Acknowledge anything you are doing or thinking that doesn't bring honor to the Father, and repent of (turn away from) that sin and turn to Jesus.

- **ASK.** This is where most of us camp out with prayers, and there's nothing wrong with it. Ask for anything and everything. This is where you bring all your people and concerns.

- **YIELD.** Surrender yourself to God. If I'm in a season where something significant is going on, I go through each event, each appointment in prayer. Then wait and listen for the Holy Spirit. Embrace silent moments to be open to hearing His voice. It's tough to hear when you aren't actively listening.

- **JOURNALING.** I love journaling my prayers. Because I always have a million things spinning in my head, journaling helps me be more present. There are times when it feels a little "Dear

Diary," but journaling has been a great tool for me to converse with the Father. (Some people save their journals forever and look back to remember all that God has done. Others destroy them because what's on those pages isn't meant for anyone else to see.)

- **LET SURROUNDINGS GUIDE ME.** This is one of my favorite ways to pray with a different perspective or intention. Walk around an area such as your home, workplace, church, or neighborhood, and let what you see be a guide or prompt to pray. (Examples: You see a trash can. *Lord, I pray that you would clean out all the things in my life that aren't of you. Show me what needs to go.* You see a tree. *Father, grow me like this tree. Give me deep roots that hold me secure, and bring about much growth and vibrant life within me.*) There isn't a right or wrong way to do this; simply let what you see prompt you to pray.

- **PRAYING FOR OTHERS.** Last but not least, pray for others. I can be the worst at saying, "I'll pray for you," and having every intention to pray for the person but never doing it. Some solutions I've found helpful are to pray for them right away, lay a hand on them, or pray as I serve them. If friends share something with me, and I catch myself about to reply, "I'll be praying," I try to send a message to them, praying over them. Another trick a mentor taught me is to lay hands on someone and pray for them without them even knowing. As one of my girls grabs my hand as we walk into a store, I use that as an opportunity to pray for them. I rest my hand on my husband's back or chest as he sleeps and pray over him. Finally, another way I pray for others is while I'm serving them. When Chris and I first got married, we couldn't afford dry cleaning, so I would iron his shirts for him. As I did that, I would pray over him and speak God's truth over what he clothed himself with.

Again, there's no one right way to pray. Let your prayer life evolve with time. Just start listening and talking to God; He is listening and speaking back. Like everything else I've shared with you in this book, remember this is progress, not perfection. Prayer is how we connect personally with God, so just as each of us has a unique way of communicating with friends and loved ones, we each will have different ways of communicating with the Father.

Prayer is our way of acknowledging that we can't and trusting that God totally can. In Acts 4:31, we see the power of prayer: "When they had prayed, the place in which they were gathered together was shaken, and they were all filled with the Holy Spirit and continued to speak the word of God with boldness." That's my hope for you—that as you pray, things would begin to shake up and you'd be filled with the Holy Spirit and become bold in the things God has called you to.

Dream

> [He] is able to do far more abundantly than all that we ask or
> think, according to the power at work within us.
> Ephesians 3:20

In our family, it has felt like our hamster wheel has been spinning faster and faster than ever. Chris and I have been praying for the past few months, asking God to show us what needs to change. Where would God have our family go, do, stop, or be? We recently pulled the girls into it and had a family dream session. We gathered in a room with big windows, gave them all dry-erase markers, and told them to write out everything they wanted to do or be, each goal they had for our family. We told them to dream as if time, money, and reality weren't factors—just dream!

I'd give a prompt, and then we'd set a timer for a few minutes to dream. After the timer went off, we'd take turns sharing what we wrote. Chandler, our youngest, was beyond adorable. She said that if time, money, and reality weren't considerations, her first dream was to find a rainbow—not to see one in the sky but to find it.

Don't you love that kind of dreaming? What was wild is that she read it like it was nothing, just as confidently as she read, "No more brushing teeth" and "Go on more trips." Tucked right in the middle of really normal things, she wants to find a rainbow. Oh, to dream like Chandler! I want that for you; I want that for myself!

And let me tell you something: as her parents, we will do everything we can to bring her to a rainbow. She didn't even know she was being audacious; she simply dreamed up what she'd love to do or be and laid it out there for her mom and dad. As her mom, I take so much delight in that. As you brainstorm, show yourself self-compassion, as we discussed in the chapter about loving yourself. As you dream, ask yourself what a loving mom or dad would say about your dreams. You might be unable to imagine your parents that way, and I'm so sorry if that's true. But you could probably imagine how loving parents might respond—that is how the Father wants to reply to you.

With all this, let me also say that just because Chandler's dreams were so endearing, that doesn't mean that we will do everything on her list. Because we love her so very much, we will still make her brush her teeth because that's best for her. Also, as someone who loves to pack a bag and go on any adventure, I'd love to take her on vacation tomorrow. The truth is we will have to wait until the calendar and the budget allow it. Sometimes even good and possible things are delayed because the timing, while not ideal, is better later.

As a life coach, this is the step I love and thrive in—brainstorming and strategy sessions are my superpowers. I've found that many of my clients are stuck so much in the day-to-day that they never dream. At first a large part of my job with clients is helping them get off the hamster wheel of their lives—spinning like crazy but going nowhere. Dreaming and brainstorming about your purpose or what you could do doesn't mean you will do it. That is just part of the process. Sometimes imagining what could be opens us up to the "but God can" transitions in our stories simply because we begin to see the possibilities.

I want to walk you through a few things to reflect on as you begin to dream.

What in your life brings you much joy—that you've done in the past or currently do?
This is to help identify some of the parts that have worked.

What in your life has brought a lot of stress and has drained you—again, from your past or currently?
This is not to say that what you do won't be hard—things that are worth it are always hard. But there is a difference between hard and totally draining.

Who are some people you admire and see yourself doing something similar to?
Mark next to each person what it is specifically that you admire about them.

If you could be or do anything, what would that be?

No disqualifying allowed! This is your safe place to process.

Many of us are relatively good at processing questions or thoughts similar to this at the beginning of the year or on birthdays. However, we don't know what this looks like regularly. Some are naturally disciplined and able to stick with whatever goals come from dreaming. The rest of us need a lot of help. First, I'd recommend setting up a monthly meeting with yourself. Just as prayer isn't a one-and-done thing, we must keep dreaming and continue implementing changes in our lives from those dreams. Second, accountability is everything. Get a friend or several friends and do these exercises together. Then check in regularly with one another on progress and struggles. If you don't have any friends right now who would be interested in going through these exercises with you, keep looking. Maybe a counselor, life coach, or mentor could come alongside you. Let others in; let them help you. It's good to have someone else's perspective in your life.

You don't have to choose between prayer and dreaming. You are stronger when you do both. Our prayers anchor us to the Father and help us seek His purposes for our lives. And our dreaming allows us to see what is possible and helps us connect the dots of where God has already been moving in our lives. But when we dream of what could be and pray to the Father, we get to experience God doing what He can do! That's when we see our mountains move.

Now go do some of those things! You obviously can't do everything, but what could you do? This is where you combine prayer and dreaming; submit these all to God and ask Him to show you what is His will and what is a good idea but not for you right now. This is where you will choose to trust God. Next I'll guide you through how to wait, take baby steps, and make giant leaps of faith.

Pray

Father, help me with this process! Show me how to pray; I feel foolish for even praying about knowing how to pray. But Lord, I want to grow in prayer and learn to talk with You, not just talk at You. And show me how to listen and hear You. Help me to trust You with these next steps. Give me a bigger vision for my life than I'm capable of dreaming up myself.

Process

1. Where are you on prayer—do you get stuck praying while you wait for the right time, or do you rush past it? What's one goal you can set to make prayer a foundational part of your life?

2. How could you incorporate prayer into your everyday life? Are there people you can learn from by asking them what their prayer life is like?

3. Looking back at the dream section, does anything stand out to you? After our family brainstorm, we all starred one thing that was our top priority. Is there one part that stood out to you that you want to think is your priority?

4. What keeps you from praying or dreaming? What distractions or thoughts limit those?

Hearers & Doers Challenge

Gather a few friends or your family and brainstorm as a group. Brainstorms are always better with others than alone because you get fresh and outside perspectives. Invite others to pray for you, and share your list of dreams with others to see if they have any thoughts.

18

WAIT, BABY STEP, LEAP OF FAITH

> Never be afraid to trust an unknown future to a known God.
>
> Corrie ten Boom

My girls have all been competitive dancers, and as odd as this sounds, one thing I've loved most about dance is how it teaches them progress, not perfection. They've learned they can't do it on their own, nor can they do it perfectly the first (or hundredth) time. To dance at their elite level means hours of training and practice each week—both in technique and the dances they'll compete months and months after learning them. It's doing the same thing over and over and over and over again. It's failing hundreds of times before you succeed. Thomas Edison, inventor of the light bulb, was on to something when he said, "I have not failed 10,000 times. I have not failed once. I have succeeded in proving that those 10,000 ways will not work. When I have eliminated the ways that will not work, I will find the way that will work."[1] My girls are learning through dance that things don't come easily; most things take a lot of time and hard work. It's a lot of two steps forward and one step back. For each new skill or dance style they want to learn, they've had to go to countless classes, practice at home, and sometimes even get private lessons. They've fallen and gotten concussions and broken bones, and they get way less sleep than they should at their age. And they've absolutely loved it and dominated at competitions!

Their bravery, not to mention their talent, mesmerizes me. They step onto that stage with three judges sitting just feet away, each with a microphone in their hand as they record critiques while the girls perform their routines. Can you imagine dancing that close to three judges who are sharing how you could be better? Months of practice all come down to those two minutes. What tenacity they've built to dance confidently, knowing they could still be better. I want to giggle through half their dances and sob through the other half. Seeing Karis, Moriah, and Chandler shine up on that stage makes this mama's heart burst with pride.

I want you to approach this—learning to wait, take baby steps, and make giant leaps of faith—the same way my girls have to approach dance: remembering progress, not perfection. None of this is intended to shame you, nor is it a list to become legalistic about. These are merely suggestions, some hard-learned advice on what has worked for me and what hasn't. Remember that two steps forward and one step back is still progress. Also remember that figuring it out is hard, and you might be tempted to quit because easier seems so much better. Friend, don't stop where you are, and don't miss what God can do in your life. On your own, you can't . . . *but God* absolutely *can*!

Jesus often taught in parables, sharing stories with a lesson folded in. While I'd heard the parable of the talents (Matthew 25:14–30) before, I don't think I ever truly connected with it as I did a few years ago. You already know that comparison is a struggle for me. Due to some perceived and actual failures at the time, I was in a serious state of comparison, leading to all kinds of self-pity. Around this time is when I truly heard the parable of the talents.

This parable is about a man going on a long trip who chose a few trusted workers to manage some of his wealth. To one he gave five talents; to another, two talents; and to another, one talent, each "according to his ability." (v. 15; For context, a talent is equivalent to about twenty years of the average salary.) The one who had received five talents immediately started trading with them, and he was able to earn five more talents. Also, the one with two talents got to work and doubled his talents. But the one who had one talent wasn't sure what to do. Fearing that he'd mess things up, he dug a hole and hid the talent.

Finally, after some time had passed, the master returned and settled accounts with his workers. The one who had been given five now had ten, and the master said, "Well done, good and faithful servant. You have been faithful over a little; I will set you over much. Enter into the joy of your master" (v. 21). The same happened with the man with two talents, who brought his master four talents. And the master said to him, "Well done, good and faithful servant. You have been faithful over a little; I will set you over much. Enter into the joy of your master" (v. 23). Then the one who had received just one talent came forward. He shared that he had been afraid, so he hid the talent and handed the master what had been his—the one talent. The master replied, "You wicked and slothful servant" (v. 26). The master questioned why he didn't at least put it in the bank to gain interest. He took the one talent from that man and gave it to the worker who had made ten.

I was wallowing in extremes. I envied people who had been given "five talents," turned them into ten, and even got a bonus talent. Then I was placing myself in the position of the worker with one talent who then lost everything. The truth is that while there had been a season of my life when I had hidden out of fear, I wasn't in that place anymore. I had been stepping into places where God was calling and leading me. He had done wild things I couldn't have imagined—so many "but God can" moments. And there were also plenty of setbacks. I'm learning that setbacks aren't indicators of failure or being on the wrong path. Sometimes they are God's way of giving you experience or teaching you a lesson that makes you ready for what is to come.

When I heard this parable, I assumed that the servant with the most was the best and the one with the least was the worst. Because we know that the master wasn't happy with the servant who ended up with no talents and was pleased with the worker who had the most, this is where I was a little frustrated with God. Why did he give more to the one who already had the most? In my envy and comparison, I felt like everyone who already had so much kept getting more. It didn't seem fair. (I'm embarrassed to admit this, but I hope sharing it helps someone.) Then the Holy Spirit guided me to look again at the parable, and I noticed that the master's response to the servants with ten and four talents was the same. They both were called good and faithful servants. They both had been faithful over a little, they both were getting set over more, and they both were able to enter the joy of their master. Sure, one now had four talents and the other had eleven, but it does not seem like the master cared about the results; he cared about faithfulness.

That's when I sensed the Lord asking me, *Will you be faithful with your two even if it means you only end up with four?* This woke me. I can't say that I no longer struggle with envy or comparison, but I can tell you the struggle is far less since this realization. I am far more content with my four talents. Truthfully, I'm less focused on the number and more focused on being faithful to God and what

He has entrusted to me. I want all of us to bring as much as possible so I can cheer on those who bring more and encourage those hiding their talents.

It's time to come out of hiding! Don't focus on the number of talents you've been given; just be faithful with what you have. If you aren't sure what your talent is yet, no worries. Many people don't know their purpose; they often find their way into it. Not to mention that our purpose, God's intention for our lives, is ever-evolving. I'd encourage you to take the following steps as you decide to trade and invest your talents.

Wait

They who wait for the LORD shall renew their strength; they shall mount up with wings like eagles; they shall run and not be weary; they shall walk and not faint.

Isaiah 40:31

In chapter 18 on prayer, I said that sometimes we get stuck praying as a form of hiding. While that is true, waiting on God isn't the same as hiding. Also, waiting doesn't mean doing or thinking nothing. For my dancer daughters, waiting means they are auditioning for the team and then waiting to see if they made the cut. While they are waiting, they keep dancing and training. Waiting is a necessary part of any process. If, as soon as they made the team in May, they decided to head to a competition the next month, they wouldn't be ready. While it sounds fun to perform right away, it would simply be too soon. However, we've often confused waiting with doing nothing, and that is simply not waiting.

Waiting can be frustrating, but most good things take time to grow. We need to be busy planting seeds, watering them, and tending to the soil. One day, soon or possibly far off, seeds will sprout and grow, then blossom into what will become a stunning bouquet of flowers. Don't rush past the waiting—it's where you grow. It's where you begin to experience living a *But God Can* life instead of settling for what you can make happen.

Waiting is doing less of what you can do and pausing to see if it's what God wants you to do. Waiting is quieting your life to make space to hear from God. Sometimes we miss Him because we are so busy trying to do things on our own.

Do you need to wait on anything you've been rushing?

Is there any way you are actually hiding under the cover of "waiting on God"?

Hiding often shows up as "I'm praying about it" or "When God makes it clear, then I'll do X."

Baby Step

Trust in the LORD with all your heart, and do not lean on your own understanding. In all your ways acknowledge him, and he will make straight your paths.

Proverbs 3:5–6

Marathon runners who start off sprinting generally end up having a difficult race, which is why pacing themselves is so important. Living out your purpose in life is a marathon; it is not a sprint. You've likely heard Aesop's fable "The Tortoise and the Hare." The tortoise consistently crawled through the race while the hare sprinted, napped, sprinted some more, and got distracted. Who won the race? The one who was consistently inching forward. Your baby steps might seem small now. You might feel like you are getting lapped, but each step adds up if you keep going.

It's okay to take your time as long as you aren't being disobedient in doing so. Ask God what your next baby step is. Sometimes this is very clear, and sometimes it feels a bit more like you are guessing. The guessing part keeps most of us from ever taking that first baby step. We don't want to get it wrong. I understand that. But, friend, we must trust in God's goodness that if we take a baby step in faith and it ends up being one in the wrong direction, He will lovingly lead us back. We fear the punishment or disappointment of God more than we trust in the goodness of a loving Father who always wants to lead us back to His way.

If you are genuinely unsure of your next step, I recommend talking to a good friend, family member, or mentor. They often are able to see in our lives what we aren't able to see for ourselves.

What's the next baby step you need to take?

You might know about thirty of the next steps you need to take, but for now focus on the very next one. Maybe it's something like taking a social media fast, breaking up with the guy you know isn't good for you, or saying yes or no to something.

Leap of Faith

> Have I not commanded you? Be strong and courageous. Do not be frightened, and do not be dismayed, for the LORD your God is with you wherever you go.
>
> Joshua 1:9

There will be times when the next thing you need to do isn't a baby step but a giant leap of faith. I have had a few of those in my life, and I can tell you that each time has been terrifying. You feel a bit foolish when you jump without knowing exactly where you might land or if you will break something or if you will fail or if—it's the "or ifs" that keep us stuck.

No more hiding your talents, my friend. It's time to leap. Leaping is a little scarier than baby-stepping, isn't it? But that's when we get to experience God doing something that absolutely wouldn't work out if we tried it on our own. Before you consider the leaps you need to take, think through the leaps you've already taken and how you've seen God move through them.

Have you taken a leap of faith in the past? How did you see God work through that leap of faith?

Before I take a leap of faith, looking back on God's faithfulness gives me confidence for the next leap. Ask the Lord to remind you of how He's been faithful to you. If you feel like you've never really leaped before, look in God's Word and note where He has been faithful to others. While those circumstances are different than yours, God never changes. What He did for others in the past, He can do for you. Also, ask others to tell you their testimonies of when they took leaps of faith. Sometimes we need to borrow the faith of others to give us the confidence to take our leaps.

Is there a leap of faith you need to take? What is it?

You are probably on the right track if what you think you should write down scares you a little bit. Again, this isn't a legal contract; you won't be bound to take this leap if it is not for you.

It's scary to leap. Hindsight is always twenty-twenty, isn't it? But when you are leaping, you feel blind, unable to see where you are going. I've shared several of my leaps with you; I can't say they get easier.

Many years ago, I was on staff at a church and, after discovering something inappropriate, I had to report the findings to those in leadership. The details of the situation aren't pertinent. We've all been there—stuck in situations where unimaginable things happen and we are faced with a choice in how we will respond. I thought the situation would be handled well. It wasn't. Months later, I ended up leaping out of that job, and a year later, we leaped out of that church. It was devastating. Ten years later, we found ourselves in a similar situation. I had to leap into confronting some things, and it didn't go well. Our family lost a lot . . . again; we were hurt a lot . . . again. As Christians, we often avoid leaps that seem negative. We don't want to deal with conflict because we feel like we should only maintain peace.

These leaps remind me of Moses repeatedly going before Pharaoh to let him know that if he didn't release the Israelites, bad things would happen (Exodus 7–12). Moses had to take some leaps going to Pharaoh. He had faith but didn't know exactly how things would work out. *But God can* make tough situations turn out for good. Sometimes it doesn't feel good, but that doesn't mean God isn't working through your leaps.

Other times when we leap, it doesn't hurt; it's too extraordinary. It's like when I decided to host a retreat for women stuck at home during the COVID-19 lockdowns. The idea came to me one night while sitting on my back porch. But it felt scary—how would I do it, who would speak at it, and would anyone even come? My first leap was to my brother, Nils, because he is my favorite person to partner with and a genius with everything online. He said he'd love to help me make it happen. Then I texted a few speaker friends, and they all said yes—fifty-five friends said yes to speak at it. And then we put a website together and shared it. I had no clue what to expect; I just knew I needed to leap. Friend, guess what? More than ten thousand women signed up. One month after that first leap on the back porch, all those women got to be encouraged by the truth when we were all facing such unprecedented times.

The outcomes of these kinds of leaps aren't always what we hope for. Think of how things worked out for Moses. All those plagues, all that conflict with Pharaoh, and now he and all the Israelites were stuck between Pharaoh's army behind them and the Red Sea in front of them. Moses took a massive leap in front of hundreds of thousands of people. I wish I could know what was going through his head as he told the people not to be afraid because God would fight for them. As he took a leap of faith and raised his staff, a wind blew in, and the sea parted. All the Israelites passed through the sea on dry ground, but Pharaoh and his army were swallowed up when the sea closed back over them.

We don't know how our leaps are going to go. We don't know if they will be painful or miraculous. But we do know that God always provides, even if it isn't how we imagined. I can't tell you how what you wrote above will go, *but God can* make a way when there seems to be no way.

I wish you could know how proud the Father is of you right now for all you've processed. If you've never had a parent look at you with eyes beaming with pride, this will be harder to imagine but so much sweeter because you'll treasure it even more. When my girls step on that stage, my heart wants to burst. I lean forward a little because I want to be as close as possible to them to take in the experience, and a smile spreads across my face. I delight in watching my girls do their thing as each expresses herself in a different way. Karis's technicality and grace make her move like liquid, taking my breath away. Moriah goes all in with every movement; there's not an ounce of hesitation in her. When she dances, you want to get up there and dance with her. And Chandler is fearless. She doesn't know her age or limitations, and she fully believes in herself, and you fully believe whatever character she plays.

All three of my girls messed up at one point during the last competition of one of our seasons. One wobbled on a turn, one forgot a move, and another fell. Can I tell you when I was the proudest of all three of my girls throughout all of their dances? It wasn't their seamless transitions, perfect turns, leaps higher than usual, expressive personality, or a hundred other things they did perfectly. It was the moments right after the wobble, blank out, and fall. To mess up in front of hundreds of people and those judges is hard. I've seen girls run off the stage in embarrassment or storm out of a theater in anger or humiliation. Without hesitation, my girls all kept dancing. They knew what they were supposed to do, who they were supposed to be, and lived that out.

The Father loves you even more than I love my girls (1 John 3:1). I know that may be hard for you to believe if you have never been lavishly loved by a parent. I'm so very sorry. *But God can* change that for you. He can love you in ways you've never known. When He sees you waiting, I picture Him leaning in with a grin spreading across His face, knowing what's to come. When He sees you taking those baby steps, I picture Him cheering for you and clapping as you begin to do your thing. When you take a giant leap of faith, I bet you take His breath away, and He is pumping His arms in the air, saying, "That's my girl!" And when you fall, then get back up again, your Father's eyes likely fill with tears of pride because He is so proud of you.

Write a letter imagining what the Father would say in response to what you answered to the above prompts about waiting, baby steps, and leaps of faith. A good test for knowing whether it's something God would say is if it sounds like something you would never write about yourself.

What might the Father's response be to what you've shared above?

Remember, your Father loves you. This is similar to self-compassion; however, this time, ask the Holy Spirit to show you what the Father might say to you about what you've processed. Write down any impressions you have. (It might help to envision a loving family member, mentor, or coach.)

Pray

Father, help me with this process! Help me to trust You with these next steps. Give me a bigger vision for my life than I can dream up myself. Show me when and how to wait—and when the waiting has become hiding. Help me to be okay with baby steps and not to worry that they are small. And also help me not to hesitate to take them because I feel I might be wrong. Instead, help me to trust You to lead me back if I get off track. Show me in what areas of my life I need to take a giant leap of faith forward, and help me to do that! Finally, I want to know what You think of all of this. Help me to hear Your voice as a loving Father would speak to His little girl.

Process

1. Do you confuse hiding with waiting? If so, what are some of your go-to signs you are hiding?
2. What's one baby step you know you need to take right now? How can you set up accountability to follow through on that?
3. Describe a time when you or someone else took a giant leap of faith and the Lord did what only He could do in that situation.
4. Was it hard for you to imagine the Father speaking to you as a loving Father would? If not, why? If so, what do you think is the cause for that?

Hearers & Doers Challenge

What are your next steps? Be clear and specific about what you should do using a bullet list. Then set deadlines for each step to make sure you follow through.

BONUS: Tell a friend about your next steps and give them permission to follow up with you.

19

GO LIVE PURPOSEFULLY AND ABUNDANTLY

Here's to the crazy ones, the misfits, the rebels, the troublemakers, the round pegs in the square holes . . . the ones who see things differently— they're not fond of rules, and they have no respect for the status quo. . . . They push the human race forward, and while some may see them as the crazy ones, we see genius, because the people who are crazy enough to think that they can change the world are the ones who do.

Steve Jobs, From the Apple Think Different ad campaign

My brother, Nils, shared the above quote by Steve Jobs with me a few years ago. I deeply resonated with it, immediately printed it off, and it's taped to my computer and my bathroom mirror. Pursuing the "but God can" to your story might make you feel like all those things—crazy, misfit, rebel, troublemaker, or a round peg in a square hole. I hope you are starting to feel less pressure to strive or perform. In addition, I pray you are beginning to experience or have greater hope for a life filled with purpose and abundance, not as the world defines either, but as God does. *But God can* take any life and change the world with it. The pressure is off, my friend! Changing the world doesn't have to be the actual world; it might just be the everyday-life world you orbit within.

You've heard a lot of my story. We've also looked at many people in God's Word who, on their own, couldn't, *but God* sure could. These were all unlikely people who couldn't on their own, *but God* still had amazing plans for them and executed them beyond their wildest imaginations.

Abraham was old, and Sarah, his wife, was barren. *But God* opened her womb, and they had a baby. God's promise that Abraham would be the father of many nations came to pass just as He said it would.

Joseph was abused and betrayed. *But God* helped him stay faithful to his purpose, content in his misplacements, and then used him to save entire nations from famine.

Moses was separated from his family, killed a man, and was afraid to speak. *But God* equipped him to free an entire people group and brought Moses into such an intimate relationship that his face literally shone from God's presence.

Rahab was a prostitute who lied to protect the Israelite spies. *But God* totally redeemed her story and made her the great-great-great-(times a lot) grandmother of Jesus.

Tamar was taken advantage of and discarded, not to mention saddled with an unjustly bad reputation for centuries. *But God* gave her the courage to stand up for herself, also placing her in the lineage of Jesus.

David was an adulterer and murderer. *But God* called him a man after God's own heart and even gave him a place in the lineage of Jesus.

Jonah ran from God.

Ruth was a widow.

Job lost all he had.

Jeremiah and Timothy were both too young.

Peter denied Christ.

The woman at the well was divorced (multiple times).

Paul persecuted Christians.

Martha worried about things.

The disciples fell asleep.

Lazarus was dead.

Thomas doubted.

The Bible is filled with examples of God taking people with all kinds of backstories and doing in their lives what only He could do. They couldn't, but God could. You can't, *but God can.*

Of all these stories, is there one that resonates the most with you? Why?

Obviously, your life differs from theirs, but is there one person you connect with more than another?

Reflect on your life. How do you feel stuck, held back, or simply disqualified?

Now use your imagination and faith and consider what God might do. Remember, talk to yourself as you would a friend. If a friend shared the below list, what might you say to them?

Now it's your turn . . .

Using the space below, write your own *But God Can* story.

First, write where you feel stuck, what is a mountain in front of you, or how you feel disqualified. Then, record what God has done, is doing, and could do!

You don't have to strive any longer. Take the burden and pressure off. God's got this, and He's got you, my friend. After sharing about his thorn in the flesh (a burden of which we don't know the details), Paul shared the Lord's response to this thorn in 2 Corinthians 12:8–10: "Three times I pleaded with the Lord about this, that it should leave me. But he said, 'My grace is sufficient for you, for my power is made perfect in weakness.' Therefore I will boast all the more gladly of my weaknesses, so that the power of Christ may rest upon me. For the sake of Christ, then, I am content with weaknesses, insults, hardships, persecutions, and calamities. For when I am weak, then I am strong."

On your own, you aren't enough. No matter what the self-help world, Christian self-help included, has told us, we know the truth. We can feel it in our core because we've tried so very hard to be enough. We know we aren't. We know we mess things up all the time. We know our attempts, while sometimes amazing, are also sometimes a big flop.

Paul said that not being enough isn't shameful but an opportunity to experience a power beyond our own. When you finally admit you are weak, you have the opportunity to experience the greatest strength possible. You can go from striving, which makes you weak and weary, to experiencing God's power, which makes you strong and enables you to live with significant purpose and abundance. You can't, *but God can*!

I love to garden. Actually, I love getting my hands dirty, being outside, and enjoying beautiful flowers. I'm not great at gardening, though, mostly because I don't slow down enough to really learn what to do. I love Knock Out roses because they are virtually indestructible—perfect for the wannabe gardener. However, even I found a way to mess them up!

Years ago I planted a few in a sunny spot in my backyard. I couldn't believe how much they grew. I loved how the bright-green leaves and vivid pink flowers made my backyard feel vibrant. Come February, when it was time to prune them back, I was very conservative. They'd grown so much I didn't want to cut them back. So I only trimmed my roses a few inches, even though they had doubled their size.

That summer my roses grew as tall as me—it was amazing! However, they were thin, only boasting three or so stalks that were super thick. While they were wildly tall, they weren't at all full. A friend told me, "Becky, you need to prune them more—you should take them to a foot tall." Anyone who loves gardening knows how this story goes. I did what she suggested, and I had different rosebushes that year. They were shorter, but there was an abundance of lush green leaves and exponentially more hot-pink roses.

I still dread February each year because I know what I have to do. My garden has grown as I add new things each year, and still, the most painful part of the year is outside in February because it's time to prune. I have no problem throwing out the things that have died—inevitably, Texas summers kill most of my potted flowers. But the pruning is brutal. Reducing those big, beautiful bushes to stubs is so sad. But Jesus said in John 15:2, "Every branch in me that does not bear fruit [my Father] takes away, and every branch that does bear fruit he prunes, that it may bear more fruit." Just as I toss out the dead plants, Jesus does the same in our lives—takes away what is dead or no longer working. The Father also knows that even the good things need to be cut back so they can grow more. Abundance often comes after seasons of cutting back.

> Is there something that needs to be pruned in your life? Does it need to be thrown out or just cut back?
>
> As you consider this, ask the Father to show you if you need to prune good things or cut away dead things.

The Enemy would love for you to believe that cutbacks are failures. Don't listen to him. Don't allow yourself to be tempted to quit. If God cuts back some things in your life, it might mean He's making a way for more growth. Oftentimes our default response to cease striving is to stop entirely. But doing nothing is not the solution. We need to find the balance between striving and living purposefully. And let's not hide behind waiting on God to make clear His plan or purpose. Let's step into it, one faith-filled step at a time, trusting that our Father is good enough to redirect our course if we get off track.

Live Purposefully

Be patient with yourself and with God. Purposeful living isn't something that just happens, nor is it just one thing. Your purpose, which you've always wanted to uncover and live out, will evolve over time just as my garden grows each year. You may take two steps toward it and one back. So give yourself grace. It will all work out, maybe not exactly as you want or expect, but it will end well. Romans 8:26–28 says,

The Spirit helps us in our weakness. For we do not know what to pray for as we ought, but the Spirit himself intercedes for us with groanings too deep for words. And he who searches hearts knows what is the mind of the Spirit, because the Spirit intercedes for the saints according to the will of God. And we know that for those who love God all things work together for good, for those who are called according to his purpose.

You aren't supposed to know exactly what to do, so you must live intentionally and openhandedly. God will show you the way; just keep taking steps toward Him. Don't let yourself get paralyzed by questioning each step. Trust the Holy Spirit within you to show you the way, and also trust Him to correct your steps if you step in a way that's not best.

It's not too late.

You aren't too far gone.

You don't know yet, *but God* does.

You aren't enough, *but God can* make you more than enough.

God tells us that each of us has a gift, and it should be used to serve others. First Peter 4:10–11 says, "As each has received a gift, use it to serve one another, as good stewards of God's varied grace: whoever speaks, as one who speaks oracles of God; whoever serves, as one who serves by the strength that God supplies—in order that in everything God may be glorified through Jesus Christ." Are you using your gift, or have you gotten distracted? Are you caught up in the hamster wheel of life, forgetting that God has said you have a gift and wants you to use it? Plus, others need you to use your talent!

I love how *The Message* translates 2 Timothy 2:20–21: "In a well-furnished kitchen there are not only crystal goblets and silver platters, but waste cans and compost buckets—some containers used to serve fine meals, others to take out the garbage. Become the kind of container God can use to present any and every kind of gift to his guests for their blessing."

Living purposefully isn't always clean and tidy. And it's rarely glamorous. We live in a society that likes quick fixes for everything—we only know life to be fast-paced. We only know strangers online through the filters they place over their faces. We are obsessed with before and afters. But when we see those two pics, we miss the countless in-between moments that weren't memorable enough to be photo-worthy.

Let's stop being so afraid of failure that we don't even try! What might you miss out on because you are afraid to discover your purpose or get your purpose wrong? Instead, let God show you—one step at a time.

There isn't one right way to live a purposeful life. Nor is God out to use you. But He does invite us to be a part of His story as we embrace our weaknesses and experience Him making us strong!

Do you have any idea what your purpose(s) might be?
Identify some possibilities. Include relationships and roles in your life. Do you have certain talents that you should put to use? Make a commitment below to take the next step with those.

Live Abundantly

Our culture has taught us that abundance is tied to material possessions and money. Sadly, this is even prevalent in many churches and ministries. It goes back to the incorrect mindset that God is a genie in a bottle ready to grant all our wishes. What a loss for those who believe this. They are missing out on true abundance! When Jesus declared in John 10:10 that Satan came to steal, kill, and destroy, He clarified that He came so we could have life and that life should be abundant. Abundant living isn't about abundant possessions or things going our way. Let's look one more time at John 10:10, but in a few translations to compare.

> I came that they may have and enjoy life, and have it in abundance [to the full, till it overflows]. (AMP)
> I came so they can have real and eternal life, more and better life than they ever dreamed of. (MSG)
> My purpose is to give them a rich and satisfying life. (NLT)
> I have come to give you everything in abundance, more than you expect—life in its fullness until you overflow! (TPT)

Abundant life does not mean that you will be rich.

Abundant life does not mean that you will be healed.

Abundant life does not mean that all your relationships will be restored.

Abundant life does not mean that you will always feel happy.

Abundance is more than this world defines it. God's Word tells us there is something better than lots of money and possessions. God brings us a better life than we dreamed of, so full it feels overflowing.

The problem many of us run into at this point is what to do when life feels anything but abundant. How do we reconcile our lack of feeling abundance with Jesus' words? The apostle Paul provided us an answer in Philippians 4:11–13: "I have learned in whatever situation I am to be content. I know how to be brought low, and I know how to abound. In any and every circumstance, I have learned the secret of facing plenty and hunger, abundance and need. I can do all things through him who strengthens me." Because of what we've experienced—abundance and want, plenty and hunger—we have the strength to do anything and know how to live content no matter the circumstance. This verse isn't saying that we can do absolutely anything. It's saying that because of what we've experienced, we can do the very thing God calls us to because He strengthens us (further confirming the truth of 2 Corinthians 12:8–10).

God never promises a perfect life. But He does offer a full and overflowing life! Oh, friend, I can't wait to see how you change your world as you stop striving, live out your purpose, and experience His abundance!

How has God brought abundance into your life outside of material possessions?
Brainstorm ways you've felt an overflow of blessing from the Lord.

Pray

Father, thank You for letting me off the hook—I'm tired of striving. Thank You for not judging my weakness but embracing it. Help me to do the same. Help me stop trying so hard and experience the power that can come when I'm weak. Show me how to live purposefully. The idea alone seems so grand and out of reach. Fill me with faith, clarity, and boldness to embrace this. Help me to take risks when I don't know what to do. When I get off course, lead me back—I trust You. Help change the way I see abundance. I want to experience the abundance You provide instead of the abundance the world promotes. Help me to give myself grace as I take two steps forward and one step back on this journey of experiencing a But God Can life!

Process

1. Was it hard to fill in the *But God Can* story? Was it hard to believe that God could do it? Go back to your answer—could you be braver and bolder with what you said?

2. How are you striving, working too hard in your own strength? How could you stop or lessen your striving?

3. What did you say your purpose is? How do you feel like you are living out your purpose? Is there anything you should stop or start doing? Do you have any beliefs that need to be corrected?

4. Finally, how have you misperceived abundance? How does the world's view of abundance differ from how the Lord defines abundance in His Word?

Hearers & Doers Challenge

What needs to be pruned in your life right now? Write out the steps that must happen, and take the first step today. (Remember that abundance can only come once we've cut back.)

BEFORE YOU CLOSE YOUR BOOK: YOUR COMMISSIONING

It is not the critic who counts; not the man who points out how the strong man stumbles, or where the doer of deeds could have done them better. The credit belongs to the man who is actually in the arena, whose face is marred by dust and sweat and blood; who strives valiantly; who errs, who comes short again and again, because there is no effort without error and shortcoming; but who does actually strive to do the deeds; who knows great enthusiasms, the great devotions; who spends himself in a worthy cause; who at the best knows in the end the triumph of high achievement, and who at the worst, if he fails, at least fails while daring greatly, so that his place shall never be with those cold and timid souls who neither know victory nor defeat.

Theodore Roosevelt, "The Man in the Arena,"
the Sorbonne, Paris, April 23, 1910[1]

I first heard this quote when *Daring Greatly* by Brené Brown was released. While Dr. Brown's book isn't Christian based, it is science based, and most everything she shares that's based on science makes a lot of sense biblically (since God created all things). A quote like this can get some of us caught up in legalism. We can say that the credit doesn't go to us when we get in the arena, but all credit is God's. Well, of course. On our own, we can't, *but God can*! But I hope you've learned that you still play a part in your story; you still need to step into the arena.

I started this book by sharing about the final hours with my mamaw. She passed later that afternoon after I wrote those words. I had your abundant life on my mind—praying, thinking, and hoping for you—as I was witnessing the end of her life. She was one of the most significant people in my world, she and my papaw. They were in my arena in the front row. Never hesitant to tell me when I had been a little too valiant. Quick to clean me up when I got dirty. And hands down the ones who set me up for success. They knew all my failings—and there have been many—but they were proud of me for getting into the arena.

One story I gut-laugh at each time I think of it is the time a scammer called my mamaw. I guess because parts of my life are online, the scammer could find enough information about me to try to pull one over on my mamaw and papaw. They called them one night and said, "Mrs. Smith, your granddaughter, Becky Kiser, has been arrested, and we need money for her bail." My mamaw was not a pushover, nor was she a fool. She told me they shared facts that all sounded legit, but she asked one clarifying question that revealed it was a con. The funniest part of this story is that my mamaw told me later, "Becky, if it had been anyone else, I would've known it was a scam, but it was you." Y'all, this wasn't the high school me she was talking about; this was the thirtysomething, college graduate, mother of three, Bible teacher me. Recalling this story used to make us laugh so hard. But in truth, I kind of like that she thought I was just wild enough to be in jail in my thirties.

I live by the motto that it can't hurt to ask or try (unless it's an obvious no—but even that feels like a good challenge). I used to be stuck in fear, saying no too often, and now I'm willing to leap into the arena. I'm not afraid to fail because I know it's all part of the process. I can identify lies much quicker now to know what's true. Because I've acknowledged I can't, my life has become so much more abundant. My life isn't perfect, but it's fruitful and full of purpose. Your life won't be perfect either. But you'll progress on the way the Lord is making for you if you don't give up. You'll produce more and better fruit than you've ever known if you don't grow complacent. And you will experience a life bursting with purpose as you wait, baby step, and take your leaps of faith.

I hope you've already begun to experience more abundance and purpose in your life as well. I know I've said it many times, but I'll say it one more time: progress, not perfection. Give yourself grace, friend—but not too much grace. Bring others into your journey and share this material with them—to hold you accountable, but also so they can experience this abundant life. As you aim to be hearers and doers of God's truth, continue to process through the chapters and questions.

The final weeks of my mamaw's life were among the sweetest, most sacred days I've ever experienced. I've never seen anyone so at peace. I sat for hours at her bedside, holding her hand and staring at her because she was stunning—peace radiating from her and a soft smile on her lips even as she slept. One day in that final week, my brother and I were on either side of her, taking in her beauty. At this point, she would wake up only for minutes at a time and then slip back off to sleep. But one time she woke up and looked at us and softly sang this hymn:

> Lead me, Lord, lead me in thy righteousness
> Make thy way plain before my face.
> For it is thou, Lord, thou, Lord only,
> That makest me dwell in safety.[2]

She sang this a few more times before she passed. Each time when she was done, she would say, "It really is true; all my life, He has led me."

You are not alone, my friend. You don't have to strive so hard to concoct an abundant life. The Lord will lead you as you continue on from this book. Even if the wilderness feels overwhelming or the desert feels dry, remember that He will make a way (Isaiah 43:19).

I am proud of you and all the work you've done. As you stop striving and choose to live purposefully and abundantly, I want to encourage you to let go of your failures, correct the ways you've been lied to, and identify what's holding you back so that you can begin moving forward. Correct negative thoughts with "but God can" truths.

~~You feel exhausted~~, *but God* makes you strong!
~~You feel stagnant~~, *but God* has a purpose for you!
~~You feel lonely~~, *but God* is with you!
~~You feel disqualified~~, *but God* makes you new!
~~You feel overwhelmed~~, *but God* sends a Helper!
~~You feel inadequate~~, *but God* says you are worthy!

As you move forward into a more purposeful and abundant life, remember to love God first and foremost. Don't forget to love yourself before you start loving others. Pray, dream, wait, take a baby step, or go ahead and take that leap of faith. Then you will begin your journey of no longer striving but living purposefully and abundantly.

Before we wrap, I would be honored to pray over you. Open up a hand or both hands and receive this commissioning:

Father, You have done so much through these pages. I'm asking that You continue to do work in my friend's life that only You can do. Continue to help her to reframe the "failures" of her past. Help her to see those as You see them. When lies creep in, speak the truth over her. Show her what plates she needs to set down and which she needs to remove. Holy Spirit, show her how to think new, true, and life-giving thoughts. When fear wants to take over, remind her of who You are. I ask that You would do what only You can—move her mountains, part her sea, make a way in her wilderness, and bring rivers in her desert. When she's exhausted, may she turn to You for strength. When she feels stagnant, reveal her next step toward Your purpose for her life. When she feels lonely, bring people into her life who can hold up her arms when she gets weary. And help her to be the kind of friend who holds others up too. When she feels hopeless, guide her to You for true comfort. When she feels disqualified, may she see that You have made her new. When she isn't sure how she can do something, help her to trust You to help her. When she feels inadequate, may she understand how worthy You see her. As she aims for progress, not perfection, help her stop striving so hard. Show her the best way to love You with all she is and has. Help her prioritize loving herself. Lead her to love others well. Give her the courage to pray and dream big. And give her clear discernment and wild faith to wait, take baby steps, and leap in faith. May she experience purpose and abundance in her life. In Jesus' powerful name, I pray. Amen! Amen! Amen!

I love you so much, my friend. While this book is coming to an end, this is just the beginning. I cannot wait to connect with you more—online and in person. Let's share what God is doing in us and encourage those around us that they can't *but God can!*

XO,

Becky Kiser

Now to him who is able to do immeasurably more than all we ask or imagine, according to his power that is at work within us, to him be glory in the church and in Christ Jesus throughout all generations, for ever and ever! Amen.

Ephesians 3:20–21 NIV

ACKNOWLEDGMENTS

Chris, you've been on this *But God Can* journey with me, not just with writing the book but in living out these concepts. We've waited, taken baby steps and made giant leaps of faith together. We've experienced a lot of pain as we've learned that God's way isn't always a rosy process or outcome. We've also experienced a far more abundant life than we ever could have dreamed. Thank you for reminding me of what's true every time I doubted I could do this. I love you . . . a lot a lot.

Girls, these words in *But God Can* are the most important things I could ever say to you. Karis, you are creative in every way, so thoughtful with your words. Your tenacity is unmatched, and your laugh is one of my most favorite sounds. While you always strive for perfection, remember you are more than enough and lavishly loved just as you are! Moriah, you have the brightest spark inside of you; your heart for others is stunning; you always work smarter, not harder; and late-night

217

talks with you are my fave. While you are a party on wheels, remember that you are wildly gifted and super talented! Chandler, you are fearlessly audacious, the sweetest and sassiest of all time. You never give up, and I hope you never stop snuggling me. While you love to perform, remember the real you is the best version of you. Girls, I love you so much . . . no matter what!

I'm grateful for my family. Love you, Mom, Dad, Robin, Tammy, Larry, Kurt, Katie, Emery, Shelby, Jason, Lexi, Hendrix, PawPaw Kiser, Bethany, and Natalie. Mamaw and Papaw, while you are no longer alive, your legacy lives on. You found your way across many of these pages. I'm so grateful to have had you both in my life in such a significant way.

Nils, you deserve your own paragraph. Bro, your belief in me and your partnership in doing ministry means more than you will ever know. So many of the leaps I felt God pushing me toward I was afraid to take on my own. *But God* has graciously allowed us to go together so many times. This book never would have been possible without you. Even more abundant days are ahead!

I feel excessively spoiled to have the most amazing community of friends. Erin, you are the sister I never had but always wanted. Your texts, Marco Polos, and breakfast dates pulled me through the wildness that was this year of writing. Kelley, goodness, was it fun to write books simultaneously with the same publisher. Thank you for putting your foot down each time I tried to quit—you've been the best cheerleader. I love that so many of the stories in these pages include you! Anne-Bennett, your friendship has been an unexpected breath of fresh air. I'm grateful for your authenticity, how present you always are, that you are the smartest person I know, and how you always bring the weird-Barbie party wherever you go. I'm really nervous I will leave someone out in my sleep-deprived writing state, but I'll give it a go: Bethany, Doylina, Elise, Emily, Kasey, Kerry, Melissa, Natalie, Paige,

Sarah, Tiffany, our OG small group, the Online Women's Ministry team, my David Elementary and Legacy Prep mom friends, my dance mom friends, and all my friends at our church.

Camp Well Summit, you've radically changed the trajectory of my life twice now. Jenn, thank you for fearlessly saying yes to God, for all the prework, and for pushing us. Cheryl, I'll never forget that day you sought me out and prayed over me; you'll always hold such a special place in my heart. Terri, you are pure fire, friend. Our amazing group cheered this book into existence, and I'm so very grateful!

Adventures of the Heart, you will see so much of what you've taught Chris and me over the years woven throughout these pages. Sandy and Reese, we are grateful for how you push us to know and hear from the Father.

I've had many counselors throughout my life, but three deserve a special shoutout because their influences are woven throughout my life and these chapters. The Bradys, you were the first ones to teach me to find safety on the couch for therapy. I am who I am today in large part because of the two of you. Ruth, you've helped me realize that I'm a truth teller and helped me learn to love myself as the Father loves me. Audra, you've taught me to see God and trust Him as a loving, present, and more than capable Father.

The Frenchie in Round Top, Texas, you were excessively generous to host me for a week to write. So many of your spaces are sacred writing spots. Deb Alexander, you were beyond generous to let me spend the final week of writing in your casita. Thank you for praying over these women and me. Black Walnut & The Kitchen, your never-ending coffee and iced tea kept me powered during early morning or late-night out-of-the-house writing sessions.

I have to say a big thanks to all the women (and a few guys) who have said yes to teaching for Online Women's Ministries (Retreat or Bible Study). It has been an honor to partner with you in ministry!

ACKNOWLEDGMENTS

I'm praying there are many good things ahead for you, my friends: Alexandra Hoover, Angie Smith, Ashley Morgan Jackson, Barb Roose, Becky Keife, Brenda Palmer, Brenda Thorn, Brittany Estes, Cami Renee Jones, Cari Trotter, Cassandra Speer, Cassie Carrigan, Cheryl Luke, Christine Hoover, Courtnaye Richard, Dani Jey, Dorina Gilmore, Elizabeth Woodson, Emma Mae McDaniel, Erica Renaud, Holley Gerth, Irene Rollins, Jamie Ivey, Jeanette Tapley, Jenn Jett Barrett, Jennifer Allwood, Jennifer Lucy Tyler, Jeslyn Foster, Jess Connolly, Julia Tucker, Kait Warman, Kara-Kae James, Kat Armstrong, Kathryn Mack, Katie Orr, Kelley Ramsey, Kia Stephens, Dr. Kim Kimberling, Kirby Kelly, Lauren Chandler, Marian Jordan Ellis, Melissa Ice, Meredith King, Michelle Myers, Molly Stillman, Natasha Ann Miller, Nicki Koziarz, Nona Jones, Oneka McClellan, Rachael Wade, Rachel Joy, Renee Swope, Sharon Hodde Miller, Simi John, Toni Collier, Vivian Mabuni, and Whitney Capps.

None of this would have been possible without my fierce, no-nonsense, on-it, and complementary literary agent, Trinity McFadden, with the Bindery Agency. You took a leap with me, advocated hard for this book, and the process blew me away.

Finally, to my W Publishing/HarperCollins team, specifically my editors, Stephanie Newton and Lauren Bridges. You are both wildly smart, uniquely creative, and incredibly encouraging. You've always considered the person who will hold this book and helped curate the words to serve them best. You've been an absolute dream to work with!

Father, may You be glorified and known more because of these words. What an honor to get to write them with Your leadership. I'll never forget this journey with You—You teaching me each lesson before it ever made it onto the pages. "Now to him who is able to do far more abundantly than all that we ask or think, according to the power at work within us, to him be glory in the church and in Christ Jesus throughout all generations, forever and ever. Amen" (Ephesians 3:20–21).

NOTES

CHAPTER 1

1. *Merriam-Webster*, s.v. "overwhelm," accessed July 23, 2023, www.merriam -webster.com/dictionary/overwhelm.
2. John Mark McMillan and Sarah McMillan, vocalists and writers, "King of My Heart," released June 23, 2015, track 3 on *You Are the Avalanche*, produced by Elijah Mosely, Meaux Jeaux Music; Raucous Ruckus Publishing; Sarah McMillan Publishing.

CHAPTER 2

1. *Merriam-Webster*, s.v. "unashamed," accessed July 23, 2023, www.merriam-webster.com/dictionary/unashamed.
2. Lee Strobel, *The Case for Christ* (Grand Rapids: Zondervan, 1998); Strobel, *The Case for Faith* (Grand Rapids: Zondervan, 2000).
3. *Merriam-Webster Thesaurus*, s.v. "abundant," accessed December 18, 2023, https://www.merriam-webster.com/thesaurus/abundant.
4. *Merriam-Webster Thesaurus*, s.v. "abundant," accessed December 18, 2023, https://www.merriam-webster.com/thesaurus/abundant.

CHAPTER 4

1. Joshua Harris, *I Kissed Dating Goodbye* (Eugene, OR: Multnomah, 1997).

CHAPTER 6

1. *Merriam-Webster*, s.v. "exhausted," accessed July 23, 2023, www.merriam-webster.com/dictionary/exhausted.

CHAPTER 7

1. *Merriam-Webster*, s.v. "stagnant," accessed July 23, 2023, www.merriam-webster.com/dictionary/stagnant.

CHAPTER 8

1. *Merriam-Webster*, s.v. "lonely," accessed July 23, 2023, www.merriam -webster.com/dictionary/lonely.

CHAPTER 9

1. *Merriam-Webster*, s.v. "disqualify," accessed July 23, 2023, www.merriam-webster.com/dictionary/disqualify.
2. Kelly Clarkson, "Kelly Clarkson—Piece by Piece (American Idol Season 15 2016) [4K]," recorded 2016, posted August 5, 2021, YouTube video, 4:50, www.youtube.com/watch?v=qmMzv9Fen_s.
3. Kelly Clarkson, "Kelly Clarkson—Piece by Piece."

CHAPTER 10

1. *Merriam-Webster*, s.v. "overwhelmed," accessed July 23, 2023, www.merriam-webster.com/dictionary/overwhelmed.
2. Bibletools, s.v. "Strong's #1586: eklegomai," accessed July 23, 2023, www.bibletools.org/index.cfm/fuseaction/Lexicon.show/ID/G1586 /eklegomai.htm#:~:text=LIBRARY%20%7C%20EMAIL%20%7 C%20ABOUT-,Greek%2FHebrew%20Definitions,choose%20 (out)%2C%20chosen.

CHAPTER 11

1. *Merriam-Webster*, s.v. "inadequate," accessed July 23, 2023, www.merriam-webster.com/dictionary/inadequate.

NOTES

CHAPTER 14

1. *Merriam-Webster*, s.v. "selfish," accessed July 23, 2023, www.merriam-webster.com/dictionary/selfish.
2. Kristin Neff, www.youtube.com/@NeffKristin.
3. Reinhold Niebuhr, "Prayer for Serenity," Celebrate Recovery, https://www.celebraterecovery.com/resources/serenity-prayer.

CHAPTER 15

1. Tom Rath, *How Full Is Your Bucket?* (Washington, DC: Gallup, 2004).
2. *Merriam-Webster*, s.v. "gossip," accessed July 23, 2023, www.merriam-webster.com/dictionary/gossip.
3. *Merriam-Webster*, s.v. "selfishness," accessed July 23, 2023, www.merriam-webster.com/dictionary/selfishness.

CHAPTER 18

1. Nathan Furr, "How Failure Taught Edison to Repeatedly Innovate," *Forbes*, June 9, 2011, www.forbes.com/sites/nathanfurr/2011/06/09/how-failure-taught-edison-to-repeatedly-innovate/?sh=3ed9c8d865e9.

CONCLUSION

1. Theodore Roosevelt, "The Man in the Arena Speech," World Future Fund, https://www.worldfuturefund.org/Documents/maninarena.htm.
2. Samuel Wesley and George Strickling, "Lead Me, Lord, Lead Me in Thy Righteousness," Trinity Hymnal, rev. ed. 1961, #727, accessed August 28, 2023, https://hymnary.org/hymn/TH1990/727.

ABOUT THE AUTHOR

Becky Kiser is tenacious in her intent to help women love God, themselves, and others. She is a life and small business coach, helping women identify and surpass their goals.

Becky is an authentic and passionate speaker at Christian women's events and retreats, as well as in prisons and in Africa. She hosts the *Hearers & Doers with Becky Kiser* podcast, interviewing new and old friends, and sharing one-on-one coaching sessions with her listeners. Becky cofounded Online Women's Ministries, which hosts Online Women's Bible Study, Online Women's Retreat, and more. Becky and her husband, Chris, live in The Woodlands, Texas, with their three daughters: Karis, Moriah, and Chandler.

Website: www.beckykiser.com

Instagram: @BeckyKiser and @OnlineWomensMinistries

Facebook: www.facebook.com/beckykiser.authorandspeaker

ABOUT THE AUTHOR

Podcast: *Hearers & Doers with Becky Kiser*
(available anywhere you stream podcasts)

To find out more about Online Women's Bible Study, Retreat,
and more, go to: www.onlinewomensministries.com

use code **'butgodcan'** for a month free!

online women's *BibleStudy*

ONLINEWOMENSBIBLESTUDY.COM

listen & subscribe to
HEARERS & DOERS WITH BECKY KISER PODCAST

available anywhere you stream podcasts.

NEED A SPEAKER OR COACH?

Fill out the form at
beckykiser.com
to have Becky come to
your next event, or to
set up a coaching call.

YOU GET SO MANY BONUSES!

To access them, go to
BECKYKISER.COM/BUTGODCAN

let's stay in touch!

I hang here
the most.
Come say hi!

 @beckykiser

f facebook.com/beckykiserllc

✉ hello@beckykiser.com